Glamour

Essays on the Art of the Theatre

Glamour

Essays on the Art of the Theatre

By
Stark Young 1881-1963

Essay Index Reprint Series

BOOKS FOR LIBRARIES PRESS
FREEPORT, NEW YORK

PN
2037
.Y63
1971

INTERNATIONAL STANDARD BOOK NUMBER:
0-8369-2099-6

LIBRARY OF CONGRESS CATALOG CARD NUMBER:
74-142712

PRINTED IN THE UNITED STATES OF AMERICA

To
David W. Prall

For permission to reprint some parts of this book thanks are due the editors of *The New York Times*, *The Century Magazine*, *The North American Review*, *The Theatre Arts Monthly*, *Vanity Fair*, and *The New Republic*.

Contents

[ix]

CONTENTS

VISITORS

DUSE

Duse's last visit to America, called to a sudden stop by her death before the end of the season, brought to our theatre an influence and quality that no words can record. Duse was not primarily and glowingly of the theatre. I should not say that she was the greatest actor that I have seen, but that she seemed of them all the greatest artist. More than any other Duse brought to the art of acting the largest and most poignant idea, the profoundest sensitivity, the deepest and most exquisite response to experience. Of all the people in the theatre she had most in common with great poetry, great joy and sorrow and beauty, great living. But her acting was, as one saw very quickly, a mere fragment of her. You got the sense in her that her art arose from her life and what she was, as the form of waves and their light and color arise from the large realm of the sea.

You never heard of Duse as you heard of Bernhardt, for example, whose splendors long since dazzled the world of men, and whose art had something about it that was easily detected as art, or at least accomplishment, by the average person. Bernhardt's genius was essentially public in its character; and there was no wit so slow or so untutored and no eye so dull as not to know that when she played, the universal elements were shaken, and passions that might have been domesticated and blurred by now became suddenly glamorous and superb. That Bernhardt was limited is obvious. She had a limited range of ideas, such ideas, for instance, as amorous seduction, pain and anger—the famous rage through tears —and the infinite throes of dying. She had certain type conceptions—limited in range though not in raw force—of the passionate, the ornate, the regal, the comic, the poetic. She had vast monotonies of temperament, however brilliant or strong. Her physical equipment—most of all the immortal voice—was extraordinary but limited in possibilities of style. Bernhardt had, too, an undiluted egotism that very often swamped the play, the other actors, and everything else save the audience's response to herself. To her all art was a passion of self, a splendor of an artist's mood, though to her, also, art was the only important thing in the world.

The public saw always that Bernhardt was a stupendous event in human enterprises. She amazed, thrilled, defeated them; she dominated even if she bored them; she delighted, exalted, and made them shiver with ice on their spines. She established, apart from herself and the moment of life that she wrought to her stage purposes, a magnificent whole idea, a popular image vastly entertaining and unforgettable, whatever else it might be, good or bad. Bernhardt had something mythical about her like a volcano. People found in her something they could recognize though they might not be able to moralize it. They could see in her a kind of sheer life principle which they could enjoy without being able to understand, something in her that the instinct of life in them drove them toward as a magnificent example of what they sensed to be the springs of all our energy and imagination—I mean elemental power.

With Duse there was no such thing. She could never have been an overpowering actress in the ordinary sense. She could not even have recited as Bernhardt was able to do, in any elaborate, heroic diction and with any of that incomparable vocal spell that Bernhardt knew how to weave. Artists over Europe were drawn to her almost unendurable tenderness and truth; in Italy her audiences alternately worshipped and railed at her. With her there was nothing audacious and spectacular, nothing violent, seductive, or world-wide. Her glamour was of another sort.

Duse was not the equal mimic in any and all styles, as Garrick seems to have been. She could never have lifted a rôle to any classic fatality and splendor as Mounet Sully could do in *Œdipus*. She had not a certain golden lustre that Ellen Terry had. She could not have exhibited that wild animality, speed, passion and impetus that Mimi Aguglia at her best moments appears to exercise without effort; as Grasso does also, and others of the Sicilian theatre. She had nothing of that romantic epic style that Chaliapin brings to Boris. She had none of the gusto and bravura of an actor like Coquelin. And Réjane had more brilliance.

Some of these qualities and accomplishments Duse obviously might have had if her nature and idea had led her to the classical heroic or the seductive or the highly veneered, the stylized, the violent, the brilliantly comic, or superbly epical. She might have crowned some tradition or school. On the contrary, however, when we come to Duse in the art of acting, it must be said that she was one of those artists, appearing from time to time in every art, who tend to break down the long and painfully built structure of the art they profess. To them their mere craft is only a clutter of old boards, rags, a necessary but obstructing shell. Their passion is truth, an immediate and urging truth in them. These artists by their labor and gifts master the domain of the art with a security and completeness that few artists professing it can ever hope to approach. But whatever craft one of these artists masters he smashes, restates, forces to vanish, scorns save only as a means to an end. Duse could never be a school or a craft, her method was herself. She would have nothing of acting for itself; she was like those who despise their bodies save only as the body disappears before the spirit within that is to be revealed. She had no tricks, no efforts to attract or pique or impress, but only the desire to exist in the life to which she had given herself for those two hours on the stage, only the desire to convey to us and to confirm for herself the infinity of living within the woman she portrayed there. This detachment and intense absorption with the truth she endured and expressed gave Duse's art its extraordinary purity, free of all exterior considerations and effects.

And so it was that you could not easily get from Duse's acting a pure acting delight. She was not the actor's actor, as Velasquez was the painter's painter, or Spenser the poet's poet. That is to say, you could not delight in her performance as supreme craft, something that delights whether it is deep or flitting, delights because of the perfection of its brush, its tone, its manner, because of its competency, because of its happy application of the art practised, because of the possibilities in it for pleasure in its sheer technical purity and perfection, regardless of everything in life outside it. Something in you withheld you from saying what a beautiful gesture that was, what a tone, what a contrivance in that scene, what reading in this, what technical facility. There was no device to rejoice in, nothing technical to extricate and set aside as a studied piece of skill; there was no eloquence, no recitation, no obvious arrangement or technical economy or evident accomplishment. All these things are good in themselves, of course; they, too, may be almost in themselves a kind of art. They are means of speaking, dialects for ideas; and, after all, art is art, not life. They lead straight toward an exhibition of style. Style, however, in the sense of an added elaboration and distinction of method, of something in itself creative and separable, style in that separable aspect of facility, skill or tact, Duse rarely had. And it was only slowly and almost unwillingly that her art would allow you an academic enjoyment; it would not yield itself to the mere choice judgments of a sophistication in taste. Duse would not grant you that kind of appreciation. It was as if she would accept no love but the love for all herself and the cost that followed.

Only slowly did you see what labor and skill had gone to make up that creation of Duse's soul in the outer forms of an art. In *Cosi Sia* you saw her bending over the child, you saw her carry the pilgrim's staff, the lines of her long garments, the pity of her hands, the wandering of her hands among the lights on the altar. You saw suddenly that dumbness and then that flutter of life through the body. You saw that the entire moment had revealed itself to you. You saw what this woman knew; and you wondered whether such a knowledge of the human life and soul resolved itself in her finally into tears or into light. But it was only gradually that you were aware of how Duse suggested perpetually a state of music which must have come from a long love and study of that art; and of how this quality was in evidence always, in her visual aspect, in the tone, and in her total conception of the part. And slowly you perceived Duse's years of familiarity with the lines of statuary, and the extent to which she had mastered from great sculpture the inevitable lines of grace and meaning, and had learned from it how to study the rhythms of the form she sought and to free these rhythms of all but that last beauty of its own characteristics.

People were numerous who objected to Duse's gestures, the rhythm of her hands, her perpetual use of draperies and arrangements of pose. To make this objection is to confuse her art with what we ordinarily recognize and require as realism. To insist on her giving up these gestures and these flowing lines is to take away one of her mediums of expression. It would be to sacrifice for mere imitative probability the possibilities of another language. Duse could find an outer image that seemed to be wholly the inner thought that she expressed. This visual statement was not a copy of something which we may see in life and from which we may guess the inner thought; no, it exhibited—as great painting does or great sculpture—a visual design as free of or as faithful to actual nature as the artist chooses to make it. To appreciate Duse's rhythms of garments and bodily movements you needed to be able to do more than recognize mere fidelity to natural human life and its ways, you had to understand the visual medium itself, to be able to see and read it, precisely as you understand music by being able to hear it and not by recognizing its resemblance to familiar sounds, to birds, bells, or stormy weather. Duse could not be understood unless one knew that these gestures and these lines were in themselves a great art; that they were added to her other mediums of expression as melody is added to the mere meaning of words.

Duse knew how to keep the mass and the line alive. She knew, like a great painter or sculptor, what degree of mere description, imitation, reproduction to put into an action, a posture, a gesture that is taken from nature; and at the same time she could give her line a life of its own, a meaning that was eventually independent of the thing she interpreted. She knew from the visual arts that no movement of gesture or line arises suddenly of itself, but that it must always exist as a part of a whole, must achieve its aptness and beauty not out of its limited, sudden self, but out of a mass of relationships; in sum, she knew what few actors know at all, that a line or gesture must begin and end. Duse knew subtly and inexplicably how to give to her very presence, to her body, as she was present on the stage, a radiance and a difference, like a creation in art. Her figure there remained in the mind as something at the same time both luminous and abstract.

And finally there was a quality in Duse's art

of which sometimes you were aware as you watched her playing, and sometimes unaware until days afterward, when the sense of it grew and filled your thoughts. This quality was the presence in what she did of mind. Not mind in the shape of a problem, an intellectual if rather obvious analysis or thesis, but a pervading thing far more profound.

You may take, for an example, the first act of Ibsen's *Ghosts*; what Duse did in it was a technical and spiritual marvel. The first act of *Ghosts* as Ibsen wrote it has an undercurrent of fine dramatic power and a sharp edge of truth. But in the course of the writing a provincialism and drabness of conception more than once appears; Mrs. Alving and her author are now and again insistent and parochial, and without either taste or imagination. Ibsen's Mrs. Alving falls into platitude, stubborn and firm. Duse turned such passages into what is not platitude, but passionate memory. What in Ibsen's lines is only half placed culturally—his reflections on life, his debates, analyses—Duse established easily in right relation to a wide culture and distinction. Meantime she set forth the idea that should dominate the play as she saw it: the idea of maternal love and of a being whose body and whose love are interposed between her son and universal law.

Ibsen's drama of *The Lady from the Sea* has turns of psychology, biology, romance, symbolic poetry, and homely comedy, beginning stalely, running into a region with deep fascination to it, and winding up in a muddle of pseudo-scientific and moralistic explanations, manias, obsessions, freedom of choice, responsibility, and the like. It is outmoded now, but much of it was always without imagination or unifying power. What Duse did with *The Lady from the Sea* was like what she had done with many another play, with Galeratti-Scotti's *Cosi Sia*, for example, in which she took the simple story of a mother who had sacrificed all for her son only to be deserted by him, and gave to it her own marvellous conception of the nature of love. It was maternal love, to be sure, that Duse expressed; but this, after all, may be the greatest love theme, since it comprises all love; it is a love that begins with the desire to create out of its own body the body of a child, and then to go on forever creating its own mind and soul in the child's soul and the child's mind. Such love underlies all life and expresses the process of all nature, which proceeds from physical substance to idea, and which within its mortal bodies creates its immortal forms and qualities.

When Ibsen's Ellida comes on the stage, with her restlessness, her hunger for the sea, her sense of the Stranger's power drawing her, we get some touch of mystery, no doubt, but also a strong suggestion of explanation; a diagnosis is suggested; the woman is neurotic, suffering from an obsession. When Duse's Ellida came on the scene what we got was a poetic idea, a thing free and complete in our minds, caught there like a light in the momentary shell of a human body. The woman was literally neurotic, yes, if you like, sick with a state of mind, exactly as we might say that she was a man's wife or breathed with her lungs. But that had little to do with the point, which consisted in the wonder of this thing felt, the singleness and purity of this mood, this dream of freedom, this affinity that affrights and allures. For this the woman there on the stage is the vessel. It is this that is permanent and beautiful and that drives forever toward the immortal; it is this that is both poetic and—and here with Duse science found its right place—that is both poetic and biological. The truth Duse discovers thus, has that oneness of life at its heights and depths that art only at its best moments can achieve.

Ibsen's play came to its final idea. The Stranger reappears. Ellida is free to choose. What Duse creates then concerns love and freedom. A complete and limitless love, she tells us, is as vast as the sea and as infinite, and is itself the ultimate human freedom. The body of Wangel stands between Ellida and the body of the Stranger who has come to take her away; the love defeats the power that has haunted and destroyed her soul. And because this love is boundless and wide and inexhaustible, it, even more than the sea, allures and affrights her and feeds and consumes her life. This love, even more than the sea, can become her mystery.

With that conception and illumination that Duse brought to the theme of Ibsen's drama the whole is lifted into poetry. She did to it what would have happened at the hands of a great poet. She threw light upon it, dilated it, discovered in it what is most significant and essential, and gave to that an existence of its own, a complete life. She discovered for it the right relation of the concrete to the ideal, of the phenomenon, the accident, to the permanent, the essential. And she created for this idea a form inseparable from it.

If Duse could dilate thus an Ibsen conception and give to it its due place in a larger cosmos of feeling and idea, her impress on the works of slighter dramatists would plainly go yet farther; it served either to remake or destroy them. To her a drama or a character exhibited only some power of life that lay in it; and so to hollow rôles, like many of Sardou's and of the ordinary theatre, she brought a devastating light; she acted out of herself some beauty and meaning that the dramatist had never imagined; and what he had not felt, of love, irony, radiance, she felt and created in the rôle.

You needed to see Duse in a shallow rôle like Sudermann's Magda or as Camille, or to watch her through a scene like that last of *The Lady from the Sea*, and then, when it was over, review and sum up what she had accomplished, if you would realize her quality. You saw then more and more that such a gradation of emphasis throughout a play, and so fine and so elusive but unforgettable a comprehension of the entire meaning of the character and theme could come only from a remarkable ability and an association with culture and ideas, combined with a poetic and reflective nature, with a grace of spirit, with a courage of mind, and, finally, with something throughout the personality, quiet and taken for granted, I mean that kind of untouched and unstressed and constant spiritual audacity that moves great natures.

Duse not only illustrated the quality of the poetic as it applies not to poetry alone but to every other art. She illustrated the nature of realism in general, especially of that best Italian realism, which is so capable of rendering by means of only actual or possible external details the inmost idea. To speak of Duse's as stark realism, as was sometimes done, makes no sense. If you observed her well you saw that she never represented or reproduced or counterfeited anything. Actions the most literal were yet removed from the actual; everything that Duse did had a certain removal and restatement to it. Every action she presented borrowed light from her.

When you know well the Greek marbles in the Naples Museum, you realize how subtly individual they are; types, yes, but within the security of the type intensely varied and singly felt. But in the north you meet with the sculpture of the younger Renaissance. You see not the type become real and individual, not, as in the classic, the poetry of the individual soul set forth with reticent intensity in universal forms. What you see is the individual reality, the very surface of the thing portrayed, set down with such spiritual and physical precision that its soul becomes its body and its body its soul. In the work of Desiderio da Settignano, Mino da Fiesole, Benedetto da Maiano and others you perceive a singular distinction in fidelity combined with ideal feeling. The portrait of the bishop at Fiesole, how much the man it is, but how removed from him and brought into our souls by the artist's taste and imperceptible style! The Guidarello Guidarelli at Ravenna, a little too direct, in the face at least too close to a mere likeness, but how full of intensity of life and animation, how full of death, too, how simply tragic and yet how subtle and elaborate in its surface planes and its comment on the young spirit within! Mino da Fiesole adds to Holbein, for example, a singular sweetness, relaxation, and grace of culture. He has an ease and poetry of distinction where Holbein has distinction of artistic conscience and character. And Rosellino's tomb for the young cardinal at Samminiato, those fine and sensitive nostrils, those still, perfect hands quieted in death, the mouth droll and clear, almost alive and yet remote with death, the modelling under the chin sagging slightly down with its own weight and yet suggesting the idea of weight rather than the sagged flesh and mere accident of it, the closed eyes and the shadows under them, the still breast with the breath now taken somehow out of it—what exact and literal truth in all this, and yet what invisible style and what distinguished approach to the actual detail, what learning and culture and reflection! And underneath all this and putting the life into it, what an endowment of sheer animal talent and vitality! This, then, can be realism; though not the realism that we have heard so much about in France, where Zola and his school have reigned and where Henri Becque and Flaubert have written their gray masterpieces; not the realism of Dutch painting, with its grotesque or brutal detail or its sound honesty, as the case might be; and not the gracious and ample realism of Velasquez. Like Dante's, though less poetic, less concrete, less intense, the realism of this sculpture is. And this was Duse's realism. It is a comment on the fact that Duse, though she was in long revolt against schools and classic formularies and almost against her craft itself, had yet no violence, no excess, and no accidents, because she kept her art close to her spirit and made sure that it expressed herself.

The poetic and realistic in Duse is further commented upon by her relation to D'Annunzio's art. D'Annunzio's gift is untranslatable into English; it is a gift for expression almost abnormal, a sensitivity to the color of experience carried beyond bounds, an abandonment to life, sensations and ideas that is in itself a kind of power. Together with these faculties D'Annunzio has a gift for style, for words. He achieves an orchestration of whatever single line he chooses to follow. It is easy to see why, and not solely for personal reasons, as people like to think, Duse followed his art and in the face of obstacles forced on the public his plays, though she knew well their dramatic defects. Her art had none of D'Annunzio's recurrent falsity or specious images. It was more ordered than his, more in scale, more wisely and sweetly seen, more sorrowfully human, more universal in meaning and appeal. But D'Annunzio's plays brought to the service of drama the poetic mind, which she not only valued as a more luminous element than some basic social philosophy or superior technic in the theatre, but knew also to be far less often found there. D'Annunzio's plays gave her a constant, beautiful release of the life in her; they poured her spirit out on things, on people, on thought; they created her over and over and lighted her genius with another.

When she talked with you Duse used to come straight across the room and sit near, her fingers sometimes touching your arm. She spoke fluently and beautifully in varied images like those of poetry and with clearly made points. She spoke of herself, her art, of you, your ideas and work, but always with a kind of deep egotism that seemed both personal and impersonal. It seemed an egotism without humor, but above the need for it, non-social but divinely human and true. It bore interestingly on her relation to artists; every one knows that the artists were numberless who drew from Duse inspiration, encouragement, fecundation of their talents; through them she became long before her death a great pathetic myth. Duse obliterated and exalted you. There was something about her central intensity that was like the creative impulse itself, like sexual love, and like creation in an artist. It was penetrating and oblivious at the same time. It ignored and held you. She reduced you to nothing and gave you at the same moment the sense of being taken as no mere individual but as something in yourself that was immortal. You felt ashamed to think of yourself or of the disconcerting oversight of your presence; and yet at the same moment you felt concerned only with what might be your eternal self. She gave you an unescapable, cruel life. You felt that after her there was no peace any more, not ever, but—in so far as you were alive at all—only the pressure and necessity and travail of creation, *la mia delizia ed erinni,* as Leonardo said of art, the delight and torment. And yet you felt the kindest humanity and affection and interest, you brought your life of small affairs to her as to a gentle, wise mother.

It is interesting that Duse's face, wonderful as it was, was even more wonderful on the stage than when seen near to. Duse had a mask that was theatrical in the highest sense. The proportions of her face had a character that organized into something even finer under the visual conditions of the stage, under the *optique du théâtre.* The space between the eyes; the definite upper lids above the dark eyes; the length of the upper lip; the proportions of the cheekbones and the brow; the ample mouth and distinct teeth, with the modelling of the chin; were all such as the light, distance, and interrelationships of the theatrical scene could bring to great expressiveness and beauty. The same was true of her voice, which gained in beauty and expressiveness when brought to the pitch and rhythm of the stage. Duse's face, seen close, was not so tragic as it looked on the stage, because of the play of interest that you could see upon it. But the immense sadness of this face came partly from the mere physical conformation, which in its sheer design was pathetic. There was also the record of pain and illness and of unfortunate or consuming events in her own experience. But over and above all these, and giving the final tragic heightening to Duse's face, was something that derived, I think, from the fact that her suffering arose most from the collision of her idealism with the mere ordinary conditions of life. From her living, her thought, and her emotion, she evolved her conceptions and ideas; and she saw these constantly defeated by the incompleteness and death in things.

Duse gave you first the impression of a certain strength, which came from the clear rhythms of her physical presence and from the ardor of her spirit when she talked. But she seemed frail too, partly from exhaustion and partly from a terrible sensitivity. Always after seeing her the thought came to you of what people from her audiences have so often mentioned, I mean the feeling she aroused of defense, the impulse to protect her. This impulse when you were face to face with her, hearing her talk, you seemed to feel less. She seemed to possess strength for her own ends and a profound vitality. But afterward, the moment you left, there grew in your thoughts a marvellous poignancy, and with it this defense of her. This, I think, arose from your feeling of the intense presence in her of that element that we know is life, fragile, poignant, necessary.

Looking at her you thought of the question, so often debated, of Duse's neglect of the advantages of make-up on the stage; and it seemed probable that she avoided elaborate make-up not only in order, as we have heard so long, to let the living written on her face be read for its own truth, not only for this reason but also because she had found that, save for a little underscoring, her mask was both too fluid and too marked to do anything but lose under paint and paste.

Duse in her last season, now past sixty, when the poverty following the war and perhaps a desire to express her art for the younger theatre had sent her back to the stage, did not suggest age so much as she suggested a diminished endurance; it was a question more of quality than quantity. That is to say, you could see clearly that the actress might not be

able to go on for so long or so many performances, or for violent scenes, but it was also
equally clear that for what she did her body
lacked nothing and was adequate in the most
exact meaning of the word. Duse kept her old
physical co-ordination; the flow of lines was
still perfect and continuous; there was no sense
of stiffness or angularity, or, as nearly always
happens with age, of that lessening in the power
of the muscles to carry out the will. The voice
was less clear and vibrant than once, but no
less dramatic and penetrating. There was still
to be heard that constant surprise and strange,
quiet vitality in rhythm which she employed
in her reading, and by which she gave, very
often without using any other means, so terrible
a sense of life. Looking at Duse's figure there
on the stage you got pretty much what you
always got, the sense of a body that had no
existence apart from its idea. As had always
been so, her art connected with her presence
as music is connected with sound.

And in one respect above all Duse triumphed.
She made no attempt to reproduce what as a
younger artist she had once done. It was no
revival of former creations, no cheating of time

and our memories that she gave. She did not strain after looking young, or paint and plaster herself into a pretty dolly, but played throughout in her own terms; she restated her dramatic material in terms of the Duse that she was at the present time, not only in appearance, but also—what is much more subtle and difficult—spiritually and mentally. In this achievement, and in the intention behind it, was illustrated, as much as in any fact about her, the nature of Duse's art and of her mind.

The same thing, I have thought, that made Duse's art illustrate the nature of all arts, made her in herself not only representative of our universal life, which is the soul, but also intensely representative in her own kind. She was, after all, profoundly Italian and profoundly feminine. She had about her something of the Italian country. That land brought by so much labor and devotion, and through so many years of work and living, to such beauty and civilization, seems after all most easy and natural and gently taken for granted. Its air and color and light, though they may be either meadows and green valleys thick with almond and olive trees, or volcanic fierce regions, harsh and touched with death, have, every day when the right hours fall, a divine sweetness come over them, often something elegiac, something that is ancient, poignant, and grave. And those towns over Italy, after long centuries of art and living, present every one of them something that is its own, and that seems to simplify all that went to make it up into at last a vivid and uninsistent whole, with its own character and truth. And everywhere in Italy the famous *combinazione* is to be seen, the faculty of taking whatever one wills out of any style or age or origin, and putting it where one pleases and adding to it whatever one likes to have added. Freedom and naturalness of choice and absence of the academic are almost the first quality in the aspect of Italian towns. And this labor, apparent ease, unity, freedom were the first quality in the aspect of Duse's art, which drew from many regions but lived always in one, and which used its culture for ends so immediate and necessary that it could not be pedantic or highly schooled.

The sweetness and harmony and poignant precision that Duse had were Italian, and a certain tragic literalness and warmth of mind.

She had the Italian consuming life, with its
simplicity and directness of approach combined with what is subtle and highly complex.
In the deepest sense Duse seemed the most
feminine of all artists. It was not so much in
the traits usually spoken of, now satirically,
now sentimentally, as characteristic of women,
it was rather something in a last fundamental
quality by which women may differ from men.
There was supremely in her that virginal or
pure quality that women have when they love
or give themselves as instruments by which,
through the birth of a child, life is created
anew. There was in Duse this quintessence of
the woman, a divine generosity, a purity of response, a beautiful singleness of mood, an absorption with living values without other considerations, an existence universal and personal
rather than social, a body and soul that are solitary and infinite with the principle of generation, a fatalism and pity that come from a nearness to birth and death.

You constantly heard and read of Duse's
sadness, of the tragic element that was said to
be always present in her, and that was admired
or resented by the spectators as the case might

be. But whether you were either depressed or left impatient, or bound forever by this, it is more profitable to think of such a quality in Duse and her art as deriving not so much from sadness as from a certain impression of finality. In her art the thing presented, the action, the thought, took on the pathos of finality, something of the far, perfect line, the hail and farewell; there was in it for us somehow a nostalgia, a tragic sense of beauty and completion.

To people for whom Duse's art was a power and a new impulse of life, her supreme quality was what lay behind no art in particular, but behind all art, the response to life. The poet, the musician, the painter and architect, and actor or dancer, and the saint, also, whose life and ways possess the continuity and creative passion of art, all draw life to them by their capacity for it. In them life is gathered, it refracts, simplifies, finds out its essential and eternal principle or idea and a new body for it, and so goes on. And in Duse of all artists people most felt the thing they most respond to in all living, an infinity of tragic wonder and tenderness.

MADAME SOREL

I⊤ was as well that the visitor to these shores from Paris should be Madame Cécile Sorel and that among her plays should be Dumas's tragedy, if it is a tragedy, of *le Demi-Monde*. Madame Sorel is an actress of the second or third rank in the French theatre and past her prime; *le Demi-Monde* is a second-rate piece, past its epoch, though still to be seen on the Paris stage. If the actress had been Bernhardt or Réjane and the play *Tartuffe* or *les Femmes Savantes* the case might be altered. These classical dramas represent a tradition, and the performance of them, in a style so expert and logical, must be expected, taken for granted. Their supreme quality might have made the method of their production seem inevitable. And the power of these greater artists than Sorel might have swept us along, more or less blindly, in whatever tracks they chose. But when a casual actress and a casual modern play come to us as Sorel came, it represents deliberate choice and supplies an excellent extreme with which to confront an alien spectator. The fundamental theatrical conceptions beneath this performance by Sorel of *le Demi-Monde* were all the more easily seen. The French tradition, the theatrical quality most characteristic of the French mind, was most clearly set forth and exposed.

The French classical theatre may be smaller in scope than the Greek. Its quality in general may have been trimmed down to the prose uses of a more limited realm of living. Its sophistication may be more trivial, its emotion often more relaxed to mere excitation, and its idealism too much softened to mere sentiment. It may have specialized itself into a limited channel, and chattered itself into something of an intellectual corner so far as European thought goes. Its whole end may be more petty and commercial than was the Greek. But the resemblance and kinship is there nevertheless. That resemblance comes out even in the acting of artists like Madame Sorel and her company, none of whom, obviously, are of the rank of the greatest French actors like Bernhardt and Mounet Sully. And it comes out even in so poor an example of French drama as *le Demi-Monde*, by Dumas fils.

The curtain rises on *le Demi-Monde*. We see

a group of persons of Parisian society and the Parisian underworld. The heroine is a woman who wishes to make an honest and profitable marriage and to change her way of living. A rich man comes back from Africa; her former lover introduces her to him. There is in the group a young girl, sophisticated but still pure or virginal, or whatever may be the neatest way of putting this intact state that she still preserves and that makes her a definite pawn in the game that this drama plays. The older woman's marriage plans all but work out; after lies, evasions, she will tell her lover the truth. But in the end she gives it all up so that the young girl may marry the man who was once this older woman's lover and who had introduced her to the African traveller's fortune.

We have no time to be puzzled over these strangely arranged events, however, for Madame Sorel enters. She spreads around her a sensation. Her walk, her manner, her gown, which is all of bands of fur and a fabric of dark rose with inwoven gold, are smart beyond words. Even her boots are to be reckoned with. She talks. Her voice is something we never hear behind our footlights. It is practised, it has a range in

pitch, in timbre; it is bright, dark; it can be
metallic, white; it can think things over without words at all but in an extraordinary hum-
ming resonance. The second act comes; more
manners. Madame Sorel wears now a gown of
bluish-green gold cloth, with panniers and silver
lace, and a cloak, hanging back as in some
charming eighteenth-century portrait, of green-
ish, indescribable blue, with a gray-fur collar.
She is golden, she is fair; her smile, her hair, her
hands, her shoulders as they shine, everything
is heightened with the lustre of Paris arts. In
the third act a marvellous pale gown, then yet
another, and another still in the last scene when
the tragic renunciation comes, a gown of gold
cloth, very dark, and a hat turned up in front,
with a lace veil over the face, covering the eyes
in fact. And there are more of the glamorous
boots. Madame Sorel has become the play almost. She moves in and out there on the scene
like a varnished pearl. She is like a manikin
from some milliner in heaven.

This play, when it moves apart from Madame
Sorel's motions, moves evidently in a world
made up for the occasion. It patters through a
Parisian atmosphere that is depraved and ideal-

istic at the same time. It paints a world that is
sordid and eloquent, short-sighted and intelligent, vain and witty. These characters on this
stage are hard, they are low, but plainly they
love beauty and especially beauty in ideas.
The gamut is run of seduction, compromising
letters, jeune fille, and a sudden and thin rhet-
oric of self-sacrifice. The conflict portrayed is
not human, it is schematic. The struggle is between the author's plan for a plot and the pup-
pets that he has invented and intends to make
carry through the plot. This play has a certain
worldly wisdom. It has no shadows, no flood
of unseen living. It has sentiment, logic, but no
creation. It has a logic of character, of events,
of desire. It does not copy life's externals, does
not set forth the actual surroundings of the
world. It does not try to reveal life's inner
truth. And yet this stage piece takes its own
course; it winds up, strikes its hour, and un-
winds.

And all this, evidently, is a result that comes
from long practice, expertness, learned economy.
As for Madame Sorel—it is plain that she is not
beautiful, or even young any more. Her face is
wide in the cheek-bones, her hair thinnish, her

mouth large. But there is the effect, nevertheless, there is all the self-possession that implies
charm, distinction, beauty. The paint, the
blond powder, the black lines running out from
the upper eyelids like a languishing portrait,
the jewels, the variety of gowns and slippers—
which the women behind you are discussing
with Madame Sorel's every appearance—all give
an effect. In the tragic places Madame Sorel,
and even these French gentlemen taking fate
in their hands with their gloves on, do seem to
give us tragic emotion. But the fact is clear
that Madame Sorel only describes or indicates
movingly the quality of tragic feeling. She does
not express it straight, but rather gives it to us
through this elaborate artifice of her craft.

All this is not the Comédie Française at its
best, that is clear. There is none of the splendid
and sonorous eloquence that declamation at its
height can achieve in Mounet Sully and his
peers. There is none of the marble and passionate restraint of fine moments on that great
stage. There is none of the grand style, the
antique dialectic, the profound resonance and
ease of action and thought. Madame Sorel's
company and their play of *le Demi-Monde*, if

taken on their lowest plane, have the finish
and excellence and vanity of soaps made in
Paris, of French food, of ordinary French prose.
On their best plane they share a great tradition. They are of the Comédie Française school,
and they afford an exposition, though slight and
pattering, of its essential place in the world of
the theatre.

What this French art of the theatre is is
urban. There is exhibited in this performance
much expressiveness, an abundance of ideas,
theories, conclusions, feelings. In it there is
nothing solitary; nothing is wholly private, but
all belongs to a society. There are no stretches
of a deep, high region of spiritual solitude.
You do not go to this out of your secret, high
realms, to be understood, to find companion-
ship, to commune with saints, and to share
your secret and incommunicable life. The art
that Sorel brings to us does not remind us of
that line in Virgil about seeming always to go
on a long way unaccompanied:

Semper longam incomitata videtur ire viam.

This art never seems to proceed from within.
It belongs to the city. Its unreal and typical

world is an invention of city minds. The reactions, the emotions, the motives that it ac-
cepts as dependable and interesting, have
evolved from years of conversation and fads
and movements. These characters that we see
there on the stage are not so divinely centred
and intense and private, but seem rather to
move in a kind of social state. From their
selves and their actions we get always the quality and rule of reason. They participate in
general passions and ideas. Our response is
most to their brains, no matter how violently
they stir and excite our nerves. Whatever hot
passion or cold plot and calculation they may
express tends to come to us directly and without impediment, straight from their brains by
way of their lips. Their lips are the red gates,
to use Homer's phrase, by which the forces of
life in them are conveyed to us.

This French tradition of Madame Sorel's
company is sophisticated rather than inspired.
It understands the relative place, the sanity
and the usefulness of enthusiasms and impulses.
It understands the perpetual current of affairs
and contacts that blunt the edge of experience
and provide substitutes and compensations for

many losses and disappointments. It is an art that depends on no illusion. Nobody pretends that this play of Dumas's is true or naïve or to be believed in. As for the necessity of illusion, we leave that to the provincials. What is asked of it is a display of themes, emotions, ideas, plots, and acting; we can enjoy these without believing that the whole is true. The whole game of this drama, this acting, this art of the theatre is admitted, it is a game with its own creative laws. Beneath its symbols people who know life and the town perceive its meanings. All things rely on mutual exchanges, common understandings, city usages.

The point of view of so urban an art rests on a sense of civilization. It will not be easily accessible to your Anglo-Saxon, who has not this instinct for the social or for the whole; morality for him has more tortuous personal meanings, very often of sex. He is capable of crusades in his own soul or in public for the good of men in a mass; he works and prays and frets for the betterment of society. He wants to make it better, but he has no particular instinct for making it more agreeable, though he may have a conscience to do so; and only theoretically does he come down out of his tower, or tree, to make himself an affable part of the general. The Anglo-Saxon common man has not the lively mentality or sheer spirits to make him social. He never easily gives up his self and the fence about it for the sake of the general pleasure; and only with labor can he keep his eye on a general opinion and harmony; only with the propulsion of loneliness, conscience, or tea, coffee, brandy, and other spiritous liquors can he tack freely over social seas. Dull or intelligent, he has something within him that throws him against life with a quiet hunger; he tends toward inhibitions for private reasons or simply for their own sake; he is romantic because of his hunger; and partly because he lacks to a certain extent taste and vivacity, he is often sentimental. He makes a comfortable and sometimes a sodden world about him; but he lives on illusions one way or another. In the opinion of his spirit there are no bounds. He is your born dreamer; and he likes to believe that his dreams are deep and important, whether anybody ever stirs by them or not, and whether they ever take any shape in his own mind or merely remain his own confused and precious inner comfort. And so it happens that he has small respect for the mind as such, he is apt to tell himself that one may have too much brains; he resents cool arrangements, frank artifice, conceded conventions and arbitrations in logical or formal styles. And he has little feeling for manners or for the surface of living; only after an intense and long culture that is possible for a few small groups alone does he become civilized as a Latin takes the word.

Civilization implies an intention that will develop in a society of individuals an art of coming together in a way that will be most agreeable to public and private interests; it implies harmony, a discipline of mutual complacency and consideration and entertainment. With the French it means that they have, on no very necessarily lofty plane, if you like, concerned themselves with evolving a mode of life that will make human society more tolerable and expert. Under such a theory things that might be merely personal adventure become contracts under the state. Individuals become members of a social order. And art manifests a desire to perfect itself for the general enjoyment and to serve the uses of society. Such a theory understands that up to a certain point art is not entirely a temperamental matter, a good deal of it can be learned. Through this, much of French art and French craft as well, though it attain no high distinction, is well adapted to the enjoyment of persons who are not by temperament or culture artistic; and so the fame of French art has spread over the world. The French have written of themselves and glorified their works till the world concedes them to be its most artistic nation. But only in this sense of a perfection on a wide and general level, of a kind of public excellence, could they support such a claim. They achieve no oftener than other races the supreme artist. But among them more than any other people in Europe the sense of art, or at least of finish, is widely applied. They make art social.

An art like this of the Comédie Française is a matter of arrangement. It is all built up. Every part is something accepted as signifying some meaning. It makes no pretension to being natural in the sense of representing nature. Its world is its own. Everything is arranged, true to a special set of principles; and the ensuing work of art has pre-eminently its own truth. Its triumphs are technical, logical, persuasively moving by means of a special language of emotion. The extent to which nature is drawn upon is arbitrary, as it is in architecture or design. And it is neither greater nor less by reason of the fact that it is consistent only with itself, with its own logic, its own artifices, rather than with some actuality outside itself. Good or bad, it is art first and last if it is anything.

The limitations of such an art of the theatre as that practised at the Comédie Française are various enough. Under its scheme of things an exact realism is impossible. We could never in this art penetrate to the last reality of some section of living by portraying the exact and revealing outward elements of it, however painful or brutal or shocking. We could not render chaos as it often stands in human experience, because chaos remains unintelligible. And most of all we are deprived of the widest chance possible to the art of the theatre for more and more inclusiveness in the expression of life. The purpose of art is to express experience, to dilate the reality of the moment, to establish upon the flux and uncertainty of things the eternal and constant fact of the idea. And it must follow that the greatest art of the theatre, the art most to be desired but never wholly attained as yet, will be that which is most free to express all things whatsoever that are in life, whether beautiful abstractions or exact images or the agonizing or the unsayable itself. The ideal art would allow for all methods of expression. Under its scheme every thought and circumstance would be allowed the form that is closest to it and that is most nearly its soul. And yet it must be said that in this French art its very limitations insure advantages.

The advantages that such an art as this of the French theatre enjoys are such as arise from the fact of its having a basis on which to construct and a more or less definite idea of society from which to observe and regulate its material. This art can fall back upon something that arises in such a society as the mind might create, upon something that we all admit as the general outline within which our experiences happen, experiences and impulses that may be warm, infinitely varied, curious, or violent, but that remain within this outline and are measured by it. As for this art of the Comédie Française, the control, the theory, the assured method and territory undoubtedly limit. But they afford a security on which the art can build an ordered and elaborate and often noble dramatic structure. By knowing its ground it approaches the ease of the immortal gods; and all that gods work, as Æschylus said, is effortless and calm. And it affords the best possible circumstances for the development of a style. Not style in that perfect sense of a vanishing and wholly revealing medium of expression, an element as simple and inevitable as a living body and the life in it; but style rather as a medium in which heightened artifice, intelligence, and emotional reality are all at one and the same time apparent, and all together delight us with something—over and above the meaning or content —of skill, distinction, and truth.

THE MOSCOW ART THEATRE

Mr. Oliver Sayler's admirable book, combined with the most intelligent and effective publicity in the course of our theatre, had made us familiar with the Moscow Art Theatre before we ever saw it. Twenty years of criticism have established the main qualities and theories of this group of artists; every one knows that their method is the representational, which professes the intention of ignoring the presence of spectators and of producing an effect of life, as life would be seen going on if the fourth wall of a room were removed; every one knows by now the phrase, "spiritual realism," implying a selection among realistic details that can bring out the inmost spirit of the actual matter. And every one knows about the exhaustive search for right particulars, the last perfection of illusion in make-up; the spirit of the group working together under Stanislavsky; the competent training that makes it possible to exchange rôles among the actors; and the sincerity of approach to the meaning of the dramatist. About

the Moscow Art Theatre these are all by now
the merest commonplaces; one may see these
players through phrases at least if not through
the eyes.

Many people saw the performances through
the phrases; they came out of the theatre de-
claring that this was the best acting in the
world. In America every year, it is true,
we hail the best thing in the world, such is
our craving for the superlative and our trust
in print. The best thing in the world comes to
us and departs, and we are ready for another
best thing in the world. But for the moment
the Moscow Art Theatre was that. The fact
that the organization was old and somewhat
tired, and some of the actors but shadows of
what they once had been, was not mentioned.
The superlative reigned, the house was crowded
in spite of a foreign language and high prices.
In the spring the company on tour returned, to
less majorities, and their visit in the following
season was by no means a triumph. I have
often wondered what these Russians thought
of that falling away after such raving heat; but
if they had known us better they would have
expected as much. The event remains, never-

theless, one of the landmarks in the history of our theatre; and the spirit and gist of it, and the qualities of it to be remembered, are never to be passed over without record.

If I had seen the Moscow company in nothing but their historical poetic drama, *Czar Fyodor*, I should have been very much disappointed. I went to *Czar Fyodor*. I saw that Moskvin was a very fine actor, with an art that was fluid, continuous, pathetic in the deepest sense. I saw that Mme. Knipper-Chekhova was a highly competent artist, and that every one in the company played carefully, freely, well. The ensembles were astonishing; as individuals and as a mass the actors in them were convincing and lifelike. And over the whole stage there was—that seven-days wonder of stage directing—a complete air of human beings living there in the familiar ways of men.

I saw a chamber in the Czar's palace, low, flat, arched, painted, gilded, with a certain beauty and barbaric splendor everywhere. These palace rooms were doubtless authentic canvases of rooms to be found in Russia, very rich and entertaining. The jewels, the costumes were magnificently rich; rubies, diamonds, gold,

and brocades stiff as flowered metal, and silks,
soft or heavy and wonderfully dyed. There
was a constant procession of these gorgeous
figures, of these tall, straight men, with their
long beards and their rich, impetuous speech;
of these women with astonishing head-dresses
and great rings and bracelets, and sweeping,
incredible mantles, everything seemingly very
correct as history goes.

The play developed. The weak Czar Fyodor,
after his father's violent reign, has come into
a kingdom that is torn by a feud between two
rival princes. His entreaties and the prayers of
the Czarina, the sister of one of these princes,
induce the two factions to make peace, and to
kiss the cross as a symbol of their agreement.
Secretly, however, they betray him. One side
plots to take away the Czarina and marry the
Czar to a princess of its party. The other side
plots to dethrone the Czar and to crown his
young son, Dmitri. The Czar, in an agony of
weakness and confusion and sick will, hesitates
and blunders on. He causes one of the princes
to be brought to trial, and takes back the other
as his counsellor. Word comes that his son is
dead, by some hidden treachery, and that

there is a war begun with the Tartars. The
Czar orders the army to the front and remains
alone with the Czarina in the cathedral porch.
Leaning against a column there he cries: "O
God, O God! Why did you make me a Czar!"

The story unfolded, more or less without
definite lines but moving along as life wavers
among mortals and their plots and purposes.
The actors in their parts looked like the very
portraits of these bygone men, like figures walking out of the sixteenth century in Russia. And
their manner, their gestures and use of the
voice, were those of every-day life as one sees
it everywhere. The groups of followers, the
mobs, were life itself; every man and all the
men together, and the court maidens, were
alive, indistinguishable, save for their antique
clothes, from people as they appear to us and
from ordinary human conduct. These were
indeed fierce, real persons there on the stage,
and what they did was what any man we know
would do if we moved him backward in time
to those events and that epoch of human experience. All these elements were easy to see
in the performance; but, except for bits of pathetic acting and for moments of pictorial

beauty of figures and garments, I cared nothing about it. I have no interest in poetry taken as prose, and almost no interest in history taken, but for its mask of antique trappings, as contemporaneous human life. For the truth of history seems to me to be a combination of actuality and remoteness. Of this sixteenth-century matter of men, equipage, and event, the reality to me is the idea of it, and this includes the vista of time as one of its chief elements. In other words, in the performance of an imperial ancient story like this of the Czar Fyodor, I should like the style of the acting to achieve, not the studied naturalness that we take daily as the ways of men, but the form, the magic of distance and scope, the conscious arrangement, the artifice and logic that would create in my mind the idea.

And I should like to see in the actor's mode of portraying these kings and princes of dead times more audacity and flight, and a hint of some ungovernable scope of feeling and thought and image, more of a kind of cosmic discovery, perhaps. And with jewels and arms and clothes I can see the merely correct history of them in museums, if I choose; what I want on the stage

is these things translated into stage terms, restated with that lustre and relief that would
make them art. We need in the treatment of
these material things the restatement that expresses our ideas of them as we see them
through the depths of time; and that expresses,
also, in terms of this historical matter our
ideas of life; that expresses even in so slight a
thing as garments an indication of idea and of
our desire for lasting elements. In sum, I
wanted through all the play less of what that
sixteenth-century situation may, or may not,
have been, and more of what to me it really
is. Chaliapin in *Boris*, then, yes, that was
another school of art that had great style, simplification, removal, magnificent idea; it remained in the mind like music, like great
poetry, great abstractions; it was independent
of every concern outside its moment, complete
in itself. As for this Moscow Art Theatre's fine
production of Alexis Tolstoy's historical poetic
drama, I was professionally attentive, admir-
ing, but quite unmoved, indifferent.

Of Gorki's play, with its mixture of the dregs
of the world, the fallen baron, the fallen actor,
the cynical philosopher, the old prostitute,

Anna the dying woman, Luka the pilgrim, and the crowd of others, and its remarkable achievement of a kind of heightened and violently crude poetic actuality, the performance seemed to me not wholly convincing but more satisfying than that of the *Czar Fyodor*. There were passages of fine directing and fine acting all the way through; that last scene of the play, for example, where the lodgers left in the place talk together, with its haunting fervor and ironic desolation; or the scene in the courtyard where the old man and his young wife talk from 'the window above to the group below, incomparable moment of pure theatre, glittering, bitter and pagan and gay, like two colors laughing together; and most of all the beautiful, faultless scenes where Luka the pilgrim ministers to the dying woman. Fine moments and some fine acting, Moskvin, Mme. Knipper-Chekhova, and Kachalov, and stretches of extraordinary poetic realism; and now and then a vast, compelling mood over all—these were the achievements of the Gorki play. But what let me down and left me dashed and disappointed was the broken quality of the performance as a whole. Too often it separated into parts. Character after character stood out to the eye, heavily accented, without a blur. Stanislavsky's Satine was the worst of these— Satine's coat, his waistcoat, his shirt, his socks, his shoes, his cap, his beard. On this general point there can be no argument, some one was wrong, either Stanislavsky or some of the other actors, Moskvin, for example, whose method was exactly contrary to Stanislavsky's; the picture Moskvin conveyed was a complete blend without obvious accentuation. Stanislavsky could not turn or move but I ran into more shreds and patches, white stitches, ragged edges, everything insufferably scored—as his speeches, for all their great intelligence, were scored—like the work of a brilliant amateur, or of an instructive coach. And too many of the events in this performance stood as brightly apart as the characters: Alyosha's entrance, for one example, where he danced into the room so delightfully in his rose-colored togs, was quite as much a "number" as anything ever seen in vaudeville. Every personage was a very portrait, perfect and unforgettable, a figure carried far beyond life, where there is more blur and less individual color and edge. All this spotting and separate rhythm and glare would be well enough so far as I am concerned; I like the effect of pure theatre frankly played as such; and I like the presentation of Gorki's play as high theatricality, which it essentially is rather than naturalism; but the possibilities in this direction were crippled by the Moscow production's working in the opposite one, working on an assumption of exact realism and the fourth-wall theory, and so mixing matters up. On the whole I came away, when the performance was over, stirred and swept and shaken in my memory as after certain great numbers on a concert programme, but with no sense of any deep mood or of one single, profound experience, either of art or of poignant life.

The two Chekhov plays were another matter! Here was that rarest of events in the theatre anywhere, the combination of acting, producing, and dramatic writing, one proceeding from another, and all illuminating one idea. Some of the players were manifestly past their prime in the actual execution of their parts—it is only intelligent to recognize that—but it mattered very little; what they did seemed forever right and fine.

Stanislavsky's Gaiev was the best of his performances; Ouspenskaya's little German governess, not an important part in the play, had tragic edge, it was a fine grotesque with a certain muted and elusive distinction beyond words. I saw there on the stage Chekhov's characterizations, so whimsical, pitiful, keen, exact; I saw Chekhov's art come true, all the strange, incessant flux of it, its quivering and exposed humanity, its vibrant and exciting minor key, its pathetic confusion of tragic, comic, inane, and grotesque. Through this performance I saw more clearly than ever how far Chekhov is from the antique world, how much he is for Rome too daring, and for Greece too dark, and how much he has of the sweetness of "wild wings that pass, that pass away." I remembered how Bianor, taking all the fatality and wholeness and humility and irony and lordly power of life, had made two lines that say everything:

This man, inconsiderable, mean, yes, a slave, this
    man is loved
And is lord of another's soul

and realized anew how the theatre of Chekhov, though it has no doubt a form in a way, remains forever without the antique finality and is essentially barbarous at its core.

No, Chekhov has no place near the sunlit Bay of Salamis, but on the burly, wistful Thames, yes. Like the Elizabethans, he, too, is non-social. In his plays he creates a contest of souls rather than of members of a society, either on earth or in the universe. To the characters in his plays ideas have no order but appear to be states of exhilaration or the axioms of tragic disgust or a babble of moods and mental exercises. The God behind these characters is vast and vague, a chaotic spirit, driving people over seas, to Paris, to fights, abasing them for their hot, black sins, lifting them up and justifying their passionate wills. Looking at this performance of *The Cherry Orchard* I saw more than ever the likeness between Chekhov's method and Shakespeare's. Shakespeare, starting with a fundamental emotion or state of mind, finds facet after facet for the surface of its expression; he makes images, comparisons, ornaments, elaborations of musical cadence, all of them springing from one source and all taken together revealing it. Shakespeare allowed himself every freedom in the poetic method, to use any flight or exaggeration or happy impossibility to secure his end. Chekhov uses only words and actions that are possible in actual daily life, that are seen and heard by the eyes and ears. As Shakespeare uses his poetic details Chekhov uses these actualities, throwing together item after item, often seemingly incongruous things, weeping, kissing the furniture, calling on memory and God, asking for water, reproaching a man for trimming his beard, in order to convey the fundamental emotion from which they sprang and which they must reveal. Without using any means that might not be perfectly possible and actual, Chekhov contrives to give us the utmost shock and centre of the life he portrays.

Shakespeare's scope and power make another discussion. Obviously Chekhov's tragedy, with its slender, gray melody, has for the Elizabethan far too much defeat; out of such a muted violence and pressure of life he does not get his tragic beauty; this is not his poetry. He will not stop with this subtle and quivering revelation of what happens when a man's vitality, and the rush and fire of it, runs into the actual world about him. The thing that concerns him is what happens when the actual world about him runs into his vitality. But, though in such diverse regions, this similarity of method between him and Chekhov is full of significance; and it appears unbelievably in the Moscow Art Theatre's interpretation. And out of this modern and realistic art I got something of the same thing that comes off from Shakespeare: the tragic excitement, the vivacity and pathetic beauty, the baffling logic of emotion, the thrill that arises from a sense of truth.

What the visit of the Moscow Art Theatre meant to the New York stage seems to be clear enough. It is not that this school or method of production is a new genre; on the contrary, this method is what we have had for a generation or more, and have tended of late to depart from. It is not that the drama that these players brought with them is in any sense new; Chekhov differs only in depth and technical perfection, not in kind, from Clyde Fitch. It is not that we have seen no acting so good as this on our own stage; in single scenes at least I have seen Jefferson, Pauline Lord, David Warfield, Haidee Wright, and others do quite as good realistic acting as any of these Russians.

It is not that the scenery of the Moscow Art Theatre can teach us anything; these settings, often battered and much mended and retained only because of the company's low finances, belong to the school of décor that we have seen carried as far as it can go by producers like Henry Irving and Belasco; and as exact realism or illusion it has, moreover, been surpassed by such settings as Mr. Hopkins' actual barroom in the first scene of *Anna Christie.*

What the Moscow Art Theatre means to our stage—apart from our delight in mere proficiency—is something that is more moral and ethical than æsthetic, in so far as morality can be distinguished from the æsthetic. Chekhov's plays carry realism to an honest and spiritual depth and candor, and to a relentless, poignant perfection and truth. These actors can act not only one scene, or one play, but, by their humility and long labor at learning the technic of their art, they are equally competent throughout many parts. They know how to project a part; when they seem to do least they are most concentric and distinct. They bring themselves to feel the character and its moods, to suffer with their own lives in it. And most of all, they have a passionate concern that, no matter how long they may act a rôle, through how many years, it may not go dead or mechanical, a mere repetition of tried details and tested stage businesses. They constantly reconsider and rehearse, almost as if the play were new to them. This does not mean that as years pass these Moscow players do a rôle better or do it worse, it means that as a school they study to do what Duse, as a single artist, could do, to keep the rôle alive in terms of themselves, in terms of what they are at the time they are playing it,—in the art of acting what an incomparable and priceless thing! The Moscow Art Theatre represents a group of sincere artists, created by their art, rich by their intense living in it, and sure of all art's importance and duration. They are artists that have been working together thoroughly and through many years, in an organization, and under distinguished and sympathetic leaders, and for a devoted public. And, most significant of all, they possess a racial or popular life from which they can draw their belief and idea.

THE PROMPT BOOK

MOVEMENT IN ACTING

WHEN you hear a man like Mr. George Copeland play Bach and afterward a Spanish habanera, you get the sense of something fundamentally musical, something that begins with the first phrase and goes on unbroken to the last note of the composition. There is no rapidity and no pause that docs not exist in relationship to what is before and after it. The whole of it is one rhythm, one magnificent and infectious continuity. Such playing of such music is like a fine piece of architecture in which the entire unity of all the parts appears and every part takes its life from the whole. The whole progression moves steadily, it is varied but unbroken.

The secret of gesture in acting lies in the fact that there is no movement and no part of any movement that means anything in itself, but only as it ensues from what comes before and proceeds into what comes after. If an actress puts her hand on a man's shoulder the mere moment of the hand's presence has no life in it and no effect. The gesture must begin in the shoulder; proceeding from the whole body, and even from the whole state of mind, perhaps, it arrives slow or fast at length at its objective. But even while it appears to rest there it carries with it the change in position by which it arrived, and it should have about it a sense of its departure from where it is. If an actor enters a room the secret of the movement of entering lies in his establishing a continuous relationship between the door from which he appears and the place that he is headed for. When that fundamental is established, the actor may walk as fast or as slow as he likes, without blurring the idea.

Chaliapin, when the ghost comes to Boris and he drops to his knees on the floor, has in reality only three or four patterns of movement; but these are so related to his entire body and so continuous among themselves that they are able to convey the immense meaning behind them. No little of the secure effect of Charlie Chaplin's pieces of business is due to the fact that, from start to finish, a scene of his possesses an unbroken flow, like music. If an actor raises his hands in supplication toward

[66]

the sky, the sense of elevation and entreaty will come not only from the gesture's flowing upward to its seeming resting-place, but also from the presence in the resting hands of their going down again to the sides; the truth of the pause exists only in the relation of the pause to what it is, in fact, but a change in movement from. Duse's bow before the curtain was expressive because it seemed not a mere bending at the hips, but rather to include everything from the feet on which she stood to the thought in her mind and the gentleness of her lowered eyelids. The purity of a gesture consists in the unmarred flow of it through the changes that are related to itself; and its purity of line is lost when these relationships are broken or confused. The average actor makes bad gestures because he can neither think nor move except in patches and unrelated instances.

Art is a process of expressing one part of life in terms of another. An architect expresses the life of his dreams and ideas in terms of his life with visual solid forms. A singer may pour into sound his erotic experience. For this reason it is true that art is not art at all except in so far as it is alive. The characteristic of the living is that it never is at rest but is a perpetual rhythm of change. A moment approaches its most complete establishment, it arrives, but even as it arrives it is breaking down into what comes after. Safe for this rhythm toward and from itself, it would be dead; it is alive only in this relative life. The same holds true of all movement on the stage; all of it derives from an unbroken rhythm of the actor's thought, and is alive only within a rhythm of the body that from the actor's entrance to his exit is continuous.

SEEING THE POINT

ONE of the commonest ideas about God is that no man could bear to look upon His face. The radiance there would be too great for mortal eyes. In an odd way the same is true of man with regard to all his experience—with objects, say, or actions or thought. He does not see the central light of experience, the essential quality that characterizes it and distinguishes it from everything else. He prefers instinctively to flee the point, to blur it over, to evade it, losing himself in a looser, easier, more elusive generality. The quality that he would willingly see in a piece of experience is a quality that may be called *a kind of a sort of a something*. And at the same time, by a yet deeper instinct, he is pursued by the essential, as he is by the idea of God; there is something in him deep down that waits for the fundamental characteristic to appear to him, to take him, to reveal the experience to him.

In art the average man is neither a poet nor a scientist; his perceptions are neither deeply poetic nor precisely realistic. He chooses a middle course which evades the point all round, giving him a little of every side without the inmost sting and shock of any. He evades the sharp comedy of things and he shrinks from their tragedy; he chooses the sentimental course, which softens, footlights and vaporizes a little whatever it touches. With the experience portrayed he is too much at home to weep to the last tragic bounds and too far from home to laugh to the depths of humor. And yet at the same time it is true, for example, that the plays that hold him finally and that survive the whims of mere seasons and single generations are those that discover in their matter a great central pattern of idea and significance, and translate this idea into all the dramatic elements involved. The power of the artist and the completeness of his performance achieve a concentration and creative life that compel men to follow and to make a great work of art a part of themselves. Meantime, however, it is true, as Plato said, that most men are blind to the fact of their ignorance of the essential character of each individual thing. They do not see in each thing that which distinguishes it from every other;

they do not see what, if the thing were freed from all but its own characteristic, would remain, and would be the point of it, and would define its existence in the midst of a multitude of things like and unlike. What men are least apt to do is to see the point.

Every man has some ability and gift toward seeing the essential quality of what he experiences. He may easily see that the characteristic of a circle is a series of points equidistant from one point. The essence of a straight line is that it is the shortest distance between any two points within it. And from such as these he passes to more difficult pieces of experience, and to the discovery of what shall be for him the essential quality of the wind at night, say, or the poetry of Shelley or Leopardi, the art of Duccio or Botticelli, the character of a great city, of heroic figures in time, or cycles of thought.

An artist, however, is, by his very nature, distinguished from most men by the force that drives him toward an essential characteristic. The extent of this force is one of the measures of the artist in him. He approaches his material —the sculptor his living model or anatomy, the painter his landscape, the dramatist his men and events—and finds in it something that is his idea; he means to discover that element which for him will be the conscious being; he finds in his material that something; he finds that which will be for him permanent and ideal, and will remain for him when the material itself has faded. Out of his own substance the artist evolves forms, ideas, as out of the growing substance of a forest the tree form evolves, and then in turn the forest form from the trees, taken together among themselves. He is driven on to creation by his desire to free his idea from the confusions and accidents of the original material and to leave it essential.

The next measure of the artist's ability, however, will be the extent to which he can carry into the terms of his art the essential that he desires to express. Any one, almost, knows how easy it is at the start to get the outside. An artist often comes early on an external and accidental semblance of what he is attempting to create. With a little talent and less instruction or practice one may paint a pleasing landscape, trees, golden sky, birds flying, or make a pretty drawing. In music a beginner with a good ear and relaxed fingers can set up a remarkable effect. And a young sculptor can catch the outside of a head, find a nose and eyes and surface planes that make a highly plausible re- sult. But only slowly does the young painter find his essential idea and the technique inevita- ble to it; only slowly the musician discovers the unescapable pattern of the musical form; and the young sculptor begins to be promising when he is unwilling to go farther than the point where he can actually carry into sculptur- esque terms, into mass and line, into solidity of form, the head that he attempts. In the art of the theatre the nearness of the means—the actor, scene, and incident—to the material— men, places, and events—makes easily possible a certain semblance of an art. But to achieve theatricality, to discover in the material some fundamental point and at the same time to ex- press that in the peculiar terms of the art in- volved, is far from easy.

The separate and individual nature of each art, and of any school or period in art, best appears through the essential idea or quality expressed in any piece of it. All arts have at bottom the same function and the same principles. But a like essential idea may be variously expressed in terms of the various parts of living, in mass and form, for example, or in color and line, or in words, or in an art that consists, as the theatre does, of light, words, places, and the movements, the voice, the bodies and presences, of human beings. The perception in a painting and in a statue, for instance, of such a like essential idea will make clear the difference between the expression of it pictorially or sculpturally, and so will in turn make clear what is essentially sculpture and what painting. It might make clear, also, how far or near to some particular experience that had been re-created in them all, the several arts may be, how available each one is for expressing the experience.

A company of artists are gathered together, shall we say, looking out over the sunset desert around the columns of Luxor. In the end the same necessity would hold for each of them, which would be to express some essential characteristic in the experience. Obviously the artist whose medium would most immediately convey the literal experience of the scene would be the painter's. He, at his peril, may set down as much or as little of the actual scene as he chooses. The sculptor would have to remove the essential idea into some less representative or photographic form; what he derived from this experience might appear in the sheer relation of abstract lines and mass. The architect might give to the lines and spaces of a façade an essence which, in the art of words, a poet might call the serenity and austere infinity of that hour and scene. And the musician, dreaming of that desert space stretching forever away from the lines of those columns in stone, might express in the unknowable depths and forces of music a kind of inmost vitality in him at that moment. Meanwhile beneath all these several pieces of art there might be one essential characteristic of the experience in that time and place; and through the perception of this in its several embodiments in the various arts the essential nature of each art might be distinguished.

In the matter of the distinguishing characteristics of the several periods and schools in any one art, the same holds true. A like essential is expressed at various periods and in various schools. The expression of the idea of saintliness, for example, or of exaltation or elegance might appear in Romanesque, Gothic, or Palladian architecture, and in Italian, Austrian, or Spanish baroque. The theme of love appears in Horace, Dante, Mallarmé and their followers. The relation of individual impulse to the general order and decorum is involved in Shakespeare, Racine, Ibsen, or Morselli. From the perception of the essential expressed so variously, the various natures of the several periods or schools may be more clearly manifest.

In all arts the elements of beauty, style, and purity have at bottom a pressing relation to the perception of the essential quality.

In any experience beauty as a pleasurable attribute appears when we perceive the characteristic quality and at the same time recognize that in the experience this quality attains to a certain unity and completeness. This is what Saint Augustine meant when he said that all beauty consisted in unity—omnis quippe pulchritudinis forma unitas est. In a work of art all beauty derives from unity in its essential character; and however great a variety of qualities may be exercised within this unity, every quality is made to relate itself to this essential.

SEEING THE POINT

All style in art begins with essential idea. When a painter says that another painter has style, or when we say that Mounet-Sully had style, we use the word in a somewhat special sense. Style in that sense means a certain heightening, a certain added elaboration, something that can be isolated from the content of the work of art though it is not false to it. Style in that sense is not necessarily the soul of the thing so much as it is the lustre of the artist. But style in any large and general sense comes back to Buffon's remark that the style was the man, or to Spenser's "soul is form and doth the body make." Style is the medium by which the idea finds expression. Style is what appears between the content of a work of art and its appearance in a form. Style is what arrives at that precise point at which the work of art comes into existence. Before this point at which it achieves its style, the work of art does not exist. In a work of art the artist has a certain underlying essential idea or characteristic in the treatment of his material, a certain point, which he sees as the soul of it. This point he puts through every part of it. Complete style arrives in a work of art only when the idea is translated into the terms of every part.

The difference between an artist and a man who has intentions but cannot create them into art, appears in the absence of the style that might accomplish this translation of idea into form. Minor artists and imitators, apart from the significance of such ideas as they possess, are what they are because they are able to put the essential characteristic not through all the parts of a work, but only in this part or that. Mr. Paul Manship, beautiful and learned as his work may often be, has a statue of a girl with fauns that we may take as an example of such incompleteness. The turn of the girl's head, the lines and folds of her garment are in the manner of the early Greek marbles; the fauns, in the management of the ears, the nostrils, the little chasings to indicate the hair above the tail, the hoofs and the eyes, remind us of that lovely pair from Herculaneum, pseudo-archaic, exotic, charming past all words. But the girl's hands and her ankles and feet are almost modern in their character; in those two details the idea that characterized the rest of the work has not found expression, and they are therefore dead, and, in fact, never lived; they are apart from the rest of the statue.

Artists that are almost wholly eclectic and not very original get the form without the content. They learn from other instances of their art and from masters of it a manner of working; they take on bodies for which they have no fulfilling souls to contribute. They take over a style which says something not their own and is almost free of them. A highly eclectic sculptor, for example, may get the surface, the external manner, the character that he has derived from another, but he cannot get the essential sculpturesque solidity which derives from the true relation of the modelled mass to its idea. And it may happen in all arts, also, that a style gets fixed, outstays its meaning; the form remains, but half the fundamental idea beneath it is lost; as at the Théâtre Français, for one illustration, where much of the tradition is, at the hands of bad actors, lacking in idea; or as in some of Michelangelo's followers, who got only his mannerisms without the ideal necessity behind them.

No style at all, then, to repeat, can arrive until the artist gets the point, the character-

istic. The completeness of the style—and of
the work of art—depends on the extent to which
this characteristic extends through every part.
An actor creating Œdipus can learn from the
play itself the character of every detail con-
fronting him. He can discern, for instance,
that his make-up requires a beard, and the
obligation for a beard will serve to comment
on his whole problem. That he must wear a
beard the actor knows not so much from tradition as from every separate aspect of the drama.
To begin with, the very story itself is not personal with Sophocles but was a racial myth
ready to his hand. This story—and the final
form of it that he uses in his play—consists
mostly of outline, a large, general pattern in
which the shadings of incident, character, and
emotional and ideal reaction are included. The
characters themselves are, first of all, types,
large forms, and afterward more or less individuals. The emotions and ideas are not so
much personal as typical, powerful visitations
within these human vessels of forces larger and
more lasting than they, passing through them,
shaking and revealing and leaving them. The
images created, the diction employed in the

play, are kept within the bounds of a certain size and a certain pattern of simplicity. From all this the actor learns, then, at the very start that his own features will too greatly individualize the rôle; just as in turn he knows, in so far as he is an artist, that the reactions he expresses, and the gestures he employs must have about them a certain outline quality, a pattern of universality; and just as in turn he knows that in his recitation he must strive for line forms rather than words and phrases, and so must move toward a sonorous and impersonal and formal manner of delivery. Sophocles as a dramatic artist succeeds and attains greatness by reason of the fact that the characteristic quality is carried greatly and completely through every part of his drama, the story, the ethical theme, the characters, the reactions, the imagery, diction, the verse. His play possesses an absolute totality in style.

The defect of Euripides, on the other hand, great poet and dramatist that he is, consists, in so far at least as the Greek dramatic form is concerned, in his not being able to create or to introduce a style that could express his quality amply or completely; Euripides leaves no little of his thought and content undramatized, un-created, and conveys it to us as more or less separable moments of literature or philosophy; it is as if Velasquez in his Surrender of Breda, instead of carrying into his very brush and into the outlines of his forms the quality that in the art of words we should speak of as gracious and most suave, had attached written words to the canvas to express further the idea in his mind.

In many a production of *The Merchant of Venice*, the casket scene has had a mass of gilding and tricking out, with every sort of detail, cushions, canopies, throne-chairs and costumes, coming and going, everything but the point; which visually is the relation of the cas-kets to the suitors, to Portia and to the whole scene; which orally is the poetic rhythm and imagery; which in sum is the pattern of idea, picture and sound that underlies the scene. In the Hopkins-Jones-Barrymore production of *Hamlet*, on the contrary, the scene where Hamlet comes upon the king at prayer was acted with the king on his knees near the front of the stage, his hands lifted to heaven. Be-hind him stood Hamlet with his drawn sword in his hand. The two figures, one behind the other, the lifted hands, the sword pointing, expressed for the eye the exact pattern of the scene's idea, the precise theme of relationships. Visually, at least, the essential of that scene had been achieved, and had been freed of every characteristic not its own.

An actor, therefore, is an artist only in so far as he can first see the point or characteristic quality and then put this through every detail of his performance. His manner, his gestures, his walk, his diction, and quality of mind will differ in *The School for Scandal* from what they must be in Ibsen's *Ghosts;* in Regnard's play of *le Légataire Universel* he will eat grapes, make love, wear his clothes or fight a duel in a style that differs from his necessary style in Beaumont and Fletcher as Regnard's precision and swift cold elegance differ from the gallantries and lyrical whimsies of the two Elizabethans. And it is through this principle that the actor will know how to approach the question of naturalness in acting, and to dispose of the usual nonsense on the subject. He will know that in acting, as in any other art, the only naturalness involved—and the only meaning that the word could have—arises from the essential nature of the work of art which he has in hand.

All purity in art begins with the translation of the essential idea. A work of art is pure in so far as it compels the ideas within it to stick to its own terms; it is pure in so far as the ideas within it find expression solely in these terms, without relying on anything else. In a work of art that is pure the idea—and every manifestation of it—discovers a body that is free of all characteristics not those of the art employed. A painting of a majestical scene or of some heroic and austere vista is not a painting at all—however stirring it may be as a visual memory or as poetry—unless this characteristic that, in the art of words, we call magnificent austerity exists in the color, the line, the brush, the composition of the picture. And so with music and every art. And that purity which we discern in the great artists' natures— and to a lovable extent in most minor artists, too—and in great saints, arises from this; what they dream and desire is for its own end and perfection, free of considerations outside itself and untouched by the intrusions of another world of aims. For them the idea or dream can alone be important; and by the side of it they are not even aware of "all other idle and unreal shapes attendant on mortality."

Criticism of art that is a matter of personal preference and individual taste and private responses is not without value, however variable these may be. But the aspect of criticism that is most constructive, useful, and not to be debated, is that which arises first from the critic's ability to perceive the characteristic quality underlying a work of art. He abstracts this characteristic from whatever embodiments of it may be apparent; he carries it to some ideal completion, and then judges the work of art by this ideal, by the extent to which this complete realization of its idea is achieved. Where the critic can do this he transcends individual accidents of mere choice. And no small part of his cultivation will derive from his training in the perception of and the acquaintance with many characteristic qualities.

And, finally, in every man the delight and happy nurture of all art—as of all other experience—will depend at length on his seeing the point, on his discovery of the last necessary

[85]

characteristic. With the growth and cultivation of this faculty he will go learning to see the point of what he considers and exercises himself upon, taking a kind of delight in finding what seems for him to be the soul of the thing observed. From the body of it the essential idea emerges like a soul; from the circle its circularity and its perfect cessation within itself; from the moonlit plain what in language he calls its stillness and infinite peace, the dream of it that there are no words to describe; from the rose its roseness, by which it lingers in the memory; from Mozart his quality, and from El Greco his; and from the poet of the *Eclogues*, the *Georgics*, and some of the *Æneid*, that character of poignant and lyrical reflection and ornate quietness that we call Virgilian. These essential qualities of things emerging out of them take on a permanence in the man's life that seems to survive them, and to achieve a kind of constancy; and so, out of the flux of all things, to offer to us something immortal in mortality.

Through this development in a man it may come to be that his pleasure in a work of art does not depend so much on the discovery of superlative instances and hot enthusiasms often soon past. It relieves him of the sense that he must acclaim the work of art as the best in the world or the best he has ever seen; and allows him the pleasure, always possible, even in an inferior thing, of discerning what the essential quality within it is and the extent to which this quality has been expressed. And in his own mind at least, if not always in the work of art, these essential ideas may dilate themselves toward perfection. This will add to that development and perfecting within himself of conceptions, qualities, essential ideas, by which not only he understands art but he lives as well. From them he gets light for his own experience, and out of his experience he adds elements to the sum of them. Art becomes— as the rest of life is—the field for his immortal search and continuity. And through this, art can reveal those in whom life is a passion of oneness and duration; and can, as Plato said of a certain music, from the divinity of its nature make evident those who are in want of the god. In great art a man seeks even more than in his own flesh a body for that which he most wishes to preserve in himself.

ILLUSION IN ACTING

THE accident of the medium employed happens in the art of acting to be the cause of many confusions in the theories of the art; and of these the worst concerns illusion.

In the art of music nobody but the simplest creature expects the sound to deceive us by making us think it a storm, or pasture bells, a waterfall, or anything whatever but music. Even if a piece of music is called *The Storm*, most people know too much to demand that the stormy sounds be heard in it always, or even from time to time. Almost any one knows that a great composer might write a piece of music about Niagara Falls that would never in the least portray the falls, but would express what might be called in words the idea of the individual's relation to the universe, or of time to eternity; and so imitate little of the roar and thunder of water. In architecture everybody knows enough not to demand that a façade look like a forest or an ocean or a turtle or a hat, or anything else in the visible world;

everybody understands that music and architecture, and some few at least that painting and poetry, are purely themselves and complete in themselves.

But in the art of acting it happens that the medium employed is very close to the result achieved. The actor who plays Hamlet is a man with a body, a voice, a mind; and so is Hamlet. A man loves, hates, fears, dies, and so does Hamlet. The resemblance in this case between the medium and the art makes a perception of the nature of the art itself more difficult. And what this does for the average man is to lead him to assume that the business of acting is to duplicate something that he has seen. He sets himself up as judge, then, in what he takes to be a matter of imitation, reproduction, verisimilitude. In this bit of art, he may tell himself, as he settles into his seat, he can feel at home.

This whole point of view and assumption falls over its own feet at many turns. In the first place it assumes that there is some fixed aspect of things, that there is always some *is*-ness for every one to see, if he can only see it; and this is by no means certain. It assumes, also, that the average man will know the perfect reproduction, the resemblance, the verisimilitude, when it arrives. But that does not hold either; for the average man does not know the color of his uncle's eyes, the tone of red roses in the moonlight, or even whether a cow's ears, though he has seen a thousand cows, are above or below the horns, or where. And lastly it assumes reproduction as the final measure of approval and the final perfection in acting, and so establishes the test of identity; the actor should not act the character, the actor should be the character. But obviously art is art, not life. The pleasure we get in art is not that it is the same thing as its subject, but that it is different. We go to see the stars floating on the waves not because they are, but because they are not, the stars in the sky. The charm of art is not duplication, but presence and absence, likeness and unlikeness. The truth of art lies not in reproduction or duplication, but in idea.

The theory of acting which demands illusion may not seem in itself so bad, since art is art, not æsthetics. If people receive the experience to be conveyed by a work of art, if they respond to it, it may not seem so important what æsthetic or moral explanation they contrive after the experience. If a man is in love it does not so much matter immediately what are the explanations and comments that he gets up about it. But in the end this explanation and theory does matter, because it affects the progress of his love and its movement toward perfection; it affects also the relation of this particular experience, this love, to the rest of his life and all life. And so the disaster about this business of illusion's being the end to be desired in acting arises from the fact that such a theory is harmful in two respects. It does not allow the artist to judge the distance from reality that he will choose to make when he sets about creation. And it leads the audience to judge a work of art by its subject-matter.

It ought to be obvious that an artist must be free to choose—always at his own peril—the degree of actuality that he wishes to preserve in his art. He can be as photographic or as conventional or abstract as he likes, always at his own risk. He may paint a tree as Gainsborough paints it, pushing natural masses toward the character of tapestry, or as Corot paints a tree, drowsy with vague mists and a dream of light, or as El Greco paints a tree, taking from it only those forms that may go up as lines and shadows in that ascending flame of his composition, or as Hokusai or some more ancient painter in China might do, seeking from the tree only a line, a pattern of nuance. It is not the distance from actuality that the tree painting must stand or fall by, but by itself, by the idea expressed in it. All of which means only that a work of art is complete in itself. You judge it first by its intention, its idea, and finally by the value or significance of this idea to you. And a work of art is art only in so far as it can be experienced as complete in itself; and—though it may gain in depth and appeal by its subject—the sheer element of art in it exists only in so far as it is essentially free of its subject.

The illusion theory blinds its fcllowers to the very first thing necessary to know of acting, which is that acting, in so far as it is an art at all, and not mere human material that on the stage remains human material and nothing else, is a language we must learn to read. In this respect it is precisely like music, painting,

or any other art. Not knowing this, people
conclude, merely because of the closeness of
the material to the result, that they can be at
home with acting; and that they need for it
only what they need in life generally, sharp
eyes, feelings, memory, and interest. To perceive acting they need to know men, places,
and events, of course, as a painter needs to
know a tree when he sees one, or a dancer to
know his legs from his arms. But these are the
barest beginnings of observation. What most
people have observed of men, places, and events
is a puny bit of knowledge indeed. If that is
what they go by in knowing acting as one of
the arts, they may as well deal with architecture also by knowing bricks from paper boxes.
The side of acting which is art and not nature
is as much of a special dialect as architecture
is, and with more difficulty isolated and learned.

People say, meaning to bestow a great com-
pliment, that an actor playing a hobo is a hobo.
If this were true, it would clearly be as good
to see the hobo and never go to see the actor
at all. People will say that when an actor as
Hamlet dies you feel that he is dead. If such
things be true it might be better to take these

characters and events as we find them in life, and go to the theatre only to see what we can see nowhere else, as we go to an aquarium to see the fish we cannot see in the pantry. But in that case we could not talk at all of illusion in the theatre; because, not being able to see elsewhere what is to be seen there, we could judge it only by what we see on the stage. Obviously—too obviously—then, an actor is not the character he acts. And the lowest form of acting—not necessarily the worst performance, of course—is mere impersonation, in so far as it tries exactly to copy the original person, which, of course, no good impersonator does. It is the same with the incident portrayed. What the actor does need not fool us by making us think that the thing is actually happening to him.

As for emotional illusion the point remains the same. In order to convey to us the emotion in its essential quality the actor must give us the effect of feeling it, otherwise the emotion is interfered with by a defect in the medium through which it is expressed. This does not imply that we must be certain that the actor at the time feels the emotion, though it should not occur to our minds at the moment that he does not; all we need is that he give us the emotion free and pure in itself; the rest is his affair. All we can ask of the actor is that he should discover what the emotion is and possess the means to convey it to us. The significant actor, like any artist in any art, uses as much actual, photographic reality and reproduction as he requires. He uses the illusion of being the character, duplicating externals, feeling the emotions, undergoing the incident, exactly as a painter uses natural objects or men. The art of acting, since it works in a material of men and actions to create actions and men, may use this duplication or reproduction more often than the other arts, no doubt, but the principle of its use is the same.

What the actor gives us is a reality and no illusion. It is truth, not lies. He creates, embodies, isolates his ideal; but he depends ultimately on no deception. He gives us an essential, the idea, the characteristic, the personage, the point, as related to itself and to life outside itself. He can simulate and counterfeit externals, but only in order to give us his truth, which does not stand or fall by the extent to

which we are fooled into believing it. When
an actor does a torture scene we are harrowed
and sickened not because we think him tor-
tured, but because we receive from him at
that moment an idea of torture so compelling
that it moves us, moves us more powerfully,
perhaps, than the sight of the same blood and
wounds in life might have done. He does not
blur any truth but that of mere accidental ex-
ternality. He does not, in so far as he is good,
blur truth at all, but isolates and intensifies it
to fuller power.

The test of acting as an art consists in the
extent to which its effect depends on some illusion that you undergo. Say, for instance, an
actress plays a scene in which a woman is beaten
and killed by her son. You can test the art of
such a scene by how much it loses its effect
upon you when on your way home you are re-
minded that it was only a play after all, that
it was not the real woman who was killed,
after all, but only the actress, who was not so
dead at this moment as to prevent her having
a cup of tea. If the pressure of the scene can
be relieved for you by such a reminder, the
acting was of small importance.

ILLUSION IN ACTING

The test of your approach to acting as an art consists—exactly as it does in painting—in the extent to which you depend on illusion for your ultimate satisfaction.

For what has come off from that scene, if it was greatly acted, in no matter what style or school, is only a greater truth; the actor gives you the eternity of love, grief, and death; you are moved as by a great building, or poem, or great music. The art of acting in that scene is ultimately to be judged by the completeness and significance of its idea. Every work of art endures at last not by its likeness to things outside itself, but by the depth and freedom of the content that it embodies and expresses.

MINOR EXHIBITIONISTS

Among our actors nowadays there is many a one who, if I should say "Remember to hold your upper lip that way when you say the word *bitter*," would turn on me with contempt or rage, meaning that I should know better than to say that sort of thing to an actor, it makes him self-conscious. And if I say to a certain young actress that she is to take the first three words in her speech staccato and raise her chin as she delivers them, she will complain that she cannot feel natural doing it that way. And if I urge another to find one particular gesture for a certain passage and, having got it, to do nothing else every night but that gesture, memorizing its exact line, I shall be rebuked as trying to make acting artificial.

I might reply to these actors that I am not so much concerned with their being natural as I am with their being interesting; I might say that an actor's business in his art is to learn to use his self-consciousness as he uses any other part of himself; I might say many other things; and it would come to little. What is

in these people's heads is the notion that acting must be themselves, and that they must
feel the thing they are trying to do, and then
act it according to their feelings. They are
taking an ingenuous view of art, a middle-
class dislike for the admission of artifice and
arrangement. They dislike to think that the
mind arranges and designs the final expression
of the moment of acting; according to them
this must arise straight from the actor's feelings at the time.

But feeling the scene is something that no
actor can forever depend on; he may upon
occasions feel the scene more or less, feel it
as before or differently, or not at all. And
even if he could be sure of the right excitement
within himself, he must remember that the art
of acting does not consist only of what is felt,
much of it lies in the external means by which
feeling is conveyed. The health of acting—as
of any other art or of life—is strictly related to
the inner experience's arriving at some outer
form, without which it never comes wholly
into being. And so it is essential that each of
these felt moments on the actor's part must
find its visual image or embodiment. In this

respect a great art in acting would share the character of nature itself; in which the form evinced—the rose, the tiger, the tree—is inseparable from the idea or soul within it; the actor's gesture would image the life within him and the life in him inform the gesture.

Obviously, however, in the acting of a dramatic moment, there are, among the various reactions that the actors may feel, some that are more enduring and significant than others. They go farther, mean more, have more content; and the definite and conscious effort to remember them and to conjure them up again may be of advantage. Meanwhile the fact remains that the process of art is one of alternate inspiration and memory. As the artist works and as he returns again and again to the work, he discovers in himself something that seems suddenly to forward the conception and revelation that his art undertakes. This happy something, often not consciously expected or prepared for, he will recognize, and will strive to remember in order that he may revive it. And so, with one discovery and invention after another, and the memorizing and repeating of them, he may bring into his final expression of the moment such radiant elements as may best create it into a form of art. Among these radiant elements there will be some that are gestures, visible bodies of the ideas working in him, and these, too, he will memorize and repeat.

The ideal for the actor would, of course, be that he should be able after due work and inspiration to arrive at some emotion or idea that discovers the profoundest quality in the dramatic moment, the deepest inclusion of life in it; and that every time he acts the moment he should, out of his great genius, recover perfectly and with luminous precision this experience; and that this truth should every time achieve exactly the gesture most capable of embodying and conveying it.

This would be ideal, and no argument about it.

But all things in life and art, as we know too well, are subject to imperfection. And the fact remains, more or less apart from all this, that for an emotion we may discover a gesture, a visual movement or line, that can take on a life of its own and can go on conveying successfully an idea to us regardless of what the actor himself may come to feel at the time he is making it. That gesture, then, will be the one that he must use. The most desirable end would be, of course, that the actor fill up the gesture whenever he uses it with the original emotion from which it derived. But often if one or the other, either the new feeling or the arranged gesture, must be sacrificed, it is better to lose the feeling and keep the gesture.

To deny this and to insist, as so many actors do, and some schools of acting also, on some direct and ingenuous relation always of what they do on the stage to what they feel in themselves at the time, is only to evince a foolish individualism and personal insistence; and to suffer from a kind of exhibitionism by which you will to show yourself willy-nilly; and to make your art the immediate exhibition of whatever you are at the moment, as if it were yourself and not the moment that is the thing to be shown.

This insistence is not only vulgar and insignificant; it shows an ignorance of the essential character of form and of the nature of all art and all creation, which is constantly releasing forms that possess their own separable and independent life and meaning.

[102]

And finally there is something uncultured and barbarous in this whole attitude. The physical body achieves forms and forces that can bridge it over the times when it is not functioning at its best; a man achieves ideas and moral conceptions that carry him over the inequalities and saggings of his mental and moral existence; men in societies achieve laws and systems that sustain the life of the group when conditions falter; and so with the achievements of sustaining forms in an art. Culture, as distinguished from mere instinct and inprovisation, begins with the knowledge of this fact.

There was a moment in *Œdipus Rex* as Mounet-Sully played it when Œdipus is reduced to the last despair; everything has been taken from him, his honor, his children, his mother and wife, his kingdom and friends. And when he came to this point Mounet-Sully descended the palace steps and lay down flat on the ground. At every performance and on the same word he did that. In that gesture the whole moment was revealed; his body went back again to the bosom of the earth from which it came; he was a part of the doom and motherhood of nature; in him human life returned to its first elements. Once achieved, that gesture almost departed from any mood that the actor himself might have at any performance of the scene. It had become more important than any mood that he might have. In it Mounet-Sully had discovered a something that goes on even now in my mind as the most essential idea and tragic content of that scene. He had found what became the body of the idea, something as inevitable and complete as music.

WONDER IN ACTING

THE prosaic or unimportant actor, if he works seriously, can satisfy his audience by getting what they expect. In a scene, a line, an emotional reaction, he produces an effect that can be seen at once to be what was due; it is sensible and reasonable. And what this actor does at these satisfactory and gratifying moments is not wrong; it violates no probability but takes its place in the logical sequence of the emotion, the idea, the situation. It can be workmanlike, ample, and commendable. Such an actor will win nods of approval from all over the house. He is a good, working journeyman.

The important actor is not like this. What he does is true and satisfying, also, unless it be at times too much of a strain for people incapable of response or understanding or sympathetic energy. What this actor does also fits the sequence of the emotion, the idea, the situation. But it is never wholly expected. There is about all talent—which is the thing that makes a piece of art living instead of dead—about all

manifestations of talent, a continual slight surprise. When a real talent on the stage reads a
line or presents an emotion, we recognize the
truth of it. It is reasonable to the deepest
content of the moment. It satisfies our need for
the suitable, the fitting; but it also delights us
by something in the actor's tone, his emotional
reaction, his idea, that we had no particular
reason to expect; something that is a little
different and additional; something, indeed,
that has upon it the mystery of what is alive.

In the world of nature there is nothing—a
rose, a tiger, a tree—of which we can say that
we quite know what it is before it comes into
actual existence. By just this identity with
and this inseparability from its own creation
and birth, and by just the presence in it of
something that arrives only with its arrival, a
living thing in nature differs from a dead thing
that we might manufacture. The actor must
strive always to discover for the rendering of a
moment of his art, for a tone, a gesture, a piece
of stage business, an element of something that
could not have been foreseen or expected though
it is immediately recognized as expressive and
revealing; something that perhaps surprises

even himself, as coming from parts of himself or sources of life which are imperfectly known by him; something that comes into being only when the moment comes into being that it reveals and is. Only through this can he give us what is not alone an explanation of the dramatic moment but also the creation of it.

And so in the art of acting it is the revelation of some ultimate reasonableness rather than mere expected logic, of something luminous as well as convincing, that distinguishes talent from intention. There is always about a moment of fine acting a kind of fringe of wonder. A certain section of it, obviously, must satisfy mere daylight, reasonable expectation; must appear to explain itself; possess its rightness and propriety; it must accord to what we call, offhand, the mind, to the mind's consideration and exercise. But at either end of this plausible section it moves toward the farther reaches of our living, and it is likelife in so far as it begins and ends in wonder.

LETTERS FROM DEAD ACTORS

RACHEL TO PAULINE LORD

MADEMOISELLE—When I see you play, I am filled with remonstrance and envy, I as the great classical actress of France, you as the best actress in America for a certain kind of tragic realism.

You know my story, Mademoiselle. My father was a Jewish pedlar, a street hawker. I was four years old when my sister and I joined the troupe of Italian children that went wandering over the country singing in taverns and on the bridges; and my business at first was to go about and collect the pennies that fell to us.

When I was nine we drifted to Paris, and in the streets there I sang, a rough voice, but with such energy that the great Choron took me to his house and gave me lessons without charge. I studied at the Conservatoire, I played with no success, and at last I found a chance at the Comédie Française. Without applause I played Corneille's and Racine's heroines, until my Phèdre came and took Paris and from Paris spread my glory over the world.

Kings flattered me, authors wrote for me, the
Czar of Russia once rose to give me his seat.
It was I who stemmed the tide of Romanticism
that had arisen so hotly ten years before my
Phèdre. I gave new life to the classical art of
the French theatre. It was I who handed on
the tradition to the great Bernhardt. For fifteen
years I triumphed continuously on the French
stage until, in the summer of 1858, when I was
only thirty-seven, death came.

My genius lay in the representation of great
tragic passion, love, malignant hate, rage and
consuming despair. My method was the classical; its track was elevated, with a kind of
open and universal simplicity in its tremendous
power. My voice, which was naturally harsh,
became, with long training and labor, most even
and secure in tone, and, in its quality, tragic
and penetrating beyond words. My pallor,
my voice, my body and all its motions, my
silences, seemed when I was acting to be universal. And I set on all my art the stamp of
the great style, which was myself expressed
with distinction and magnificence.

To my classical school you, Mademoiselle,
appear to reject style. I watched for it through-

out your playing in *Anna Christie*; I watched
for it in *Samson and Delilah*, in *They Knew
What They Wanted*. Do you distrust distinction, Mademoiselle? It is all theory to you
perhaps? Or have you no way of giving yourself any grandeur, of setting free by means of
your art something superb, something that
comes off from the individual artist and goes
on existing in the world like a great thought
or pattern or idea?

In the second act of *Samson and Delilah* how
dry and unheroic you were, sitting there in
those exotic clothes of the East when you
played the actress rehearsing her rôle of Delilah! How badly you read the verse! Do you
mistrust that too, Mademoiselle, do you distrust the element of pure art added to the
natural that poetry must be? Could you not
see that convention in a work of art is only a
way of giving to it its own life, of separating
art from accident and nature?

I understand what must be your theory. If
you had told it to me in my own day, I should
have gasped. All this soiled, drab, back-alley
detail, I should have said then, what has that
got to do with art? It is not even romantic in

M. Hugo's style, I should have said. Is art to be ash-barrels and hoarse servant girls, and gin and ginger ale, as in your *Anna Christie?* Is art to be things without taste or power or beauty even in their evil or mediocrity? But why so insistently flat? I should have asked you, Mademoiselle. How stupid, I should have thought, to see you standing there without grace or elegance or fire, to see you permit yourself so colorless a presence. My body was like a marble in which some god stood and which his power moved. I should have twiddled my fingers from the end of my nose at you and laughed— as I did to the grand marquise once, not meaning her to see me, alas, as she did!—but, though I should be a street gamine still, as I always was, I should be another matter when it came to art, and from the height of that I should have scorned you.

But I am wiser now. I do not remonstrate with your theory of art, for I see now that all theories have their truth, that they are all voices of life, and that there must be some larger and more complete art in which all theories should have their place. And so now I can grant the theory of your school of acting.

RACHEL TO PAULINE LORD

It is to represent in terms of repressed emotion all that is terrible in one's life. To concentrate in your body a bitter, mute violence. To get the effect by the negative; to speak by keeping silent; to move us terribly by what you do *not* do. There was a short moment in *Samson and Delilah* when you reached a summit under this method, the moment where you crouched near the table expecting to be killed by the frenzied poet whom you had betrayed. And, in *Anna Christie*, all during the first act, with the dramatic truth of its dialogue to supply your matter, you were wonderful, Mademoiselle. You had there, in your tragic eyes and your frail body and your haunted voice, all the store of your wrongs and your suffering, you were at that moment a great artist, you were secure, inevitable. But, later in the play, which, too, somewhat failed you, after the first act, when the more positive emotions came and the pressure of a more immediate and violent life, you were not as good. What you do best so far is the backwash of violent passion, the after-mood, the parching tongue, the gray despair of that which is past but remains as a darker, inverted, inarticulate tragedy.

When later you played the little restaurant
waitress in California, who married the husband
so much older than herself, there could have
been no one who did not admire your beautiful
effacement of yourself among the players, no
one who did not feel the sweetness and goodness
created in the character everywhere and but
half said, no one who was not moved and held
by that voice that asks so little and asks so
much. But I will not say that this is enough.
Mademoiselle, though you may avoid my
school and method of art, you should yet believe that—whether or not the expression of
them in the theatre is eloquent and elevated
and removed and classical—these elements of
life are there, nevertheless, to be expressed. It
is your denials that I object to.

You should admit more into your problem.
Get more range. Keep your strange, moving
voice, if you like, where there is need for it,
but cultivate more flexibility and less monotony
of tone for much of your speaking. Cultivate
magnetism, Mademoiselle, learn to charge your
body with life when there is need of it; to make
our eyes follow it; to make it inseparable from
the dramatic moment it shares; sometimes your

body should be as negative and apart and plain-
tive as it is now; but your body should not be
always so; it should be the focus of all the life
taking place in you. Keep your theory, but
admit more to come under it.

However you may choose to express your
matter for us, believe more in the flame of things
as well as in their ashes in the soul. Study for
that; you will never be a great actress, either
realistic or otherwise, until you know it. And
in your own school you will never be great
until you know clearly one fact, which is this:
the great classical artist has to study his matter till he finds in it some large, simple pattern,
some poetry of outline, that will convey its
truth and its infinite implications; but the realistic artist, though he expresses it in terms of
the actual, has also to find his main truth and
emphasis; and he needs as much style—in his
own kind—as the classical does, as much imagination, range, variety, and a more complex if
less elevated technical expertness, before he can
find the truth.

Dear Mademoiselle, I envy you and your
modern realists many of the things that you
can do. The little homely nuance, the brutal

ugliness, the domestic, the photographic, the gentleness of the common people, the sweetness of familiar images, the lives lived in shadow or dumb byways, the daylight and prose analysis, the endless range of observation and detail. I had none of these. My talent was not for them; my school of art disdains them. To me when I lived they would have seemed trivial and unworthy of an artist, seemed of the *canaille*. My art may have been greater or less than the art you follow, but it was different.

I could and would only represent those emotions which are general, not those minute and sometimes strangely sweet or homely or sordidly accurate feelings that you can show. I could grow pale or flush, I could rave or weep or curse or pour out an impassioned love, but I could not be gray or ashen or familiar; even my sorrow had to be splendid, and my grayness a wide despair.

My art was the heroic. The region of it was in those passions that shake the world and those forces by which men's lives are nourished and consumed. You, Mademoiselle, in your best moments can be like bitter tears long since dried but more bitter than ever; your art can be like a brittle, stunned, dumb echo of some former wrong done to your soul. My soul was like a cavern from whose darkness resounds the eternal voices of the wind and sea.

LA CORALLINA TO DORIS KEANE

I saw you, Signora, in *Romance*.

I said, "What a beautiful movement! It is like a swan! An actress who knows how to walk," I said, seeing your brave, lovely motion across the stage. I heard you take our Italian voice exactly; you knew how to whiten the vowels, how to sing the tone, how to get the staccato. I heard you laugh in your *Czarina*. I saw your clear, eloquent wrists. There, I thought, is an actress with intelligence; one sees that she has a brain that can direct her body to what her will is driving at; she can point, she can put her foot down; she is not limp and sweet.

Signora, you are the only actress in America that is like me. You are like what I was when I reigned nightly at the Sant' Angelo and Venice came to see me.

Our Venice then was the summer of the world. Nobility and fashion and culture came from over all Europe to our golden city. Venice understood the world of these, she taught them, entertained them. We had five times as many theatres then as Paris had; and two hundred cafés whose doors never shut. In Venice it was eternal day. There were candles burning in the theatres, at the opera, in the grand *saloni* where the card tables were, and in the ballrooms; on the canals there were lanterns and torches where the lovers set out for Venus' Isle, and everywhere burning eyes looked out through masks.

"La Corallina," Venice called me, though my name was Maddalena Raffi. The great Goldoni said of me that I was pretty and pleasant and had a marked talent for comedy. But that was in his memoirs, written when he was gray and eighty and his flame was cold. In those happier days he adored me, he haunted my steps; in sum he could not get me out of his mind, La Corallina.

And in that one season of 1751 to 52 he wrote for me seven comedies, in all of which I succeeded. One of these plays Eleonora Duse has since taken to every European capital; *La Locandiera* was mine. As the Mistress of the Inn my triumph was such that Medebac, my rival, the wife of the manager of our troupe, grew so madly jealous that Goldoni had to write another play in which she alone might shine. But, to close the season, he wrote yet another for me, *The Jealous Women*, and in that I came off with such brilliance that poor Medebac fell into convulsions. But that was not my fault.

Not only the Venetians but the French nobles lodging in the town, the Austrian princes and the great English lords, I dazzled with my playing. I knew the world because it came to Venice. I knew the cities of Italy, for I had played in them. Bologna had been at my feet, Signora, as London has been at yours. I had my paintings, my silver tea service from the Duke of Parma, my diamond patch box from the Conte Lodovico Widiman of Padua, my lace, my fans, my court. You may have heard of how a Dalmatian prince presented to me a monkey with a coral necklace which another lover, for no love of monkeys, changed to pearls. I looked out on the world with a warm, clear wit. And the world came to see me enact my great rôles. I gave them their life as I saw it. I gave them my comment.

Signora, when you played Catherine, I could

not blame you for not expressing all you saw in the rôle. You had a public and a century that has grown middle-class and nervous about many matters. It mourns over these matters and whispers solemnly about them, or it is coarse and rowdy, but it is afraid to delight in using its wits about them. The masses have made people who ought to know better, forget that it is the play of the mind, and not the forbidden subject, that is the thing we rejoice in. In that American theatre of yours you have emotion, energy, sometimes serious thought; but you have very little pure mind and wit. Broadway should have come for a while to Venice, my dear, and made a little glittering sojourn there, but, alas, there was no Broadway then, only wide seas.

For such a public as yours Catherine and her ways of life would be raw meat, as our Brighella used to say. She is like the vindication of the nature in us all. She rips off too much veneer. She is aristocratic and barbarian at the same time; and neither of these can fit a bourgeois public. With a parterre of kings perhaps, or with M. Voltaire in the orchestra stalls—but why dream? Your brain understood Catherine very well and recognized her fantastic and comical magnificence. But you could have no hope of being free to express all you saw.

What you did in *Romance* was right. With most of your audience it passed for sentiment. They took it for the tearful story of a gay and unconventional prima donna who gave up the world for love and took to a convent. That was the chief thing in the play for them perhaps, and people must get what they can. But you saw the story with your wits about you. You put the comedy into it by knowing it was tragic, and the tragedy by knowing it was comic. One saw how well you know that humanity is always a wonderful clown, sometimes superb, sometimes absurd, but always getting the stick on its back.

You knew that this *Romance* was the drama of passionate and abundant and wilful human nature forever welling up and forever being baffled, inexhaustible, hungry, and wild. You knew that this woman's retreat to religion was only another piece of energy, and a lovable, vain search for the peace and solution that would never come. And so you found the truth by seeing the disproportion of this one soul to the conditions of life and by setting out the tragic humor of its wistful vivacity. And what you saw you had the means to express through the music and glitter of your technique.

There is already in America on the tragic side a simple feeling and form that may some day be great. In comedy there is a noisy, bubbling thing—very like the old improvised masks that Goldoni displaced with his comedy—that may come to something in time. But what your American theatre most often has is an infantile, sentimental comedy too silly to think of. Its appeal is nympholeptic sometimes, sometimes mildly moral, and always sentimental. This Syrup Comedy has its crowds. And many who are bored by it, are slow to sniff, perhaps because, as it seems to me, your Anglo-Saxon race has a respect for the mere absence of brains.

But you will never succeed at that game, Signora; you must let no prudence and no friendly advice and no long-run temptations push you toward it. You do not understand sentiment. You have a Latin mind. It is full of clear lines of wit, of daylight disillusion and the instinct for laughter. You have a kind of mystical and gentle fatality and absence. You have some of the austerity that comes of having made choices among ideas of living.

In *Romance* the lash of all this came out in your art. The precision of your beautiful romantic effects, when you played, showed a smiling mind hidden beneath them, but no sentiment. The right feeling was there, but, for those who could see, the wit also. You can never be the sort of every-day, lovable and whimsical character so dear to your public. Yours can be the comedy of distinction; or the comedy of the beloved romance of life that is lived in a rich frame; or of the trenchant worldly wisdom that tradition gives. Or you can express the comedy of a tragic and sharp mentality. And for what you can do, a public awaits you, smaller than that for the sweet high-school style, but weary with waiting for more acting in America that can make a cosmopolitan criticism of life and can paint it for those who are neither adolescent nor doting.

Signora, what I did was to make my comment on the world I saw. I had no poetry beyond that of a keen and honest eye. I had imps in my brain that saw what men and women ran after or over which they were naughty and laughable rivals. I saw the irony in power, the passionate farcicality of love, and the vanity of to-morrows. I laughed because I liked to laugh and because there was nothing else to do when you knew the end of things. And I had an honest mind that hated shams and hypocrisies and knew on the stage how to hit them off.

I adored the theatre. Goldoni and I smiled at what Monsieur Voltaire wrote to our friend the Marquis Albergati about the theatre—it was, he said, "the most divine pastime that cultivated men and virtuous women can enjoy, when more than two of them are gathered together." I smiled at that, seeing how wicked and delicious it was; but I had the same adoration. I loved the audiences and the brave show they made; the Doge himself came and Caterina Loredan, and even the Infante Don Philip of Spain.

I wanted them to think that what I did was, for all its high spirits, a picture of things. I loved their laughter and applause. But what I loved best was my own mind. And that gave a sparkling and solid unity to everything I did.

DAVID GARRICK TO JOHN BARRYMORE

Sɪʀ: Great applause has come to your Hamlet, as it did once to mine. But, as I saw you, from the start to the finish of your performance, I understood more and more that you and I set out for this creation from opposite poles. So that what you have to do to perfect your creation is precisely the reverse of what I had to do.

At the beginning my playing of Hamlet was irregular and vehement and pettish. But my performance improved almost nightly. At first I made Hamlet struggle violently with his friends when the ghost beckoned him. Later I made him remain awe-struck and motionless before the beloved spirit. At first I left out the advice to the players; I restored it later, though I always spoke it too pedantically. With Ophelia I was at first too rough and violent, with Polonius too rude. But these and other defects I softened and corrected, and at length perfected my conception of the part. Certain passages in my reading stood out always as affecting and sublime. When I taunted myself with a cowardly and pusillanimous heart, I swept the whole theatre along with me. When, by a sudden transition, I began to unfold my plan to catch the King's conscience, the house listened breathlessly. The horror and the terror of the ghostly visitation I expressed incomparably; I acted for the ghost. At the line

But break, my heart, for I must hold my tongue

I paused before the last word and dropped my arm to my side; then, with the force of the gesture, I spoke the word as if I could scarcely give it utterance. These and many other effects were universally admired. But to the last I kept some odd pieces of business, as when, for example, where Hamlet has to say that some must watch while some must sleep, I walked backwards and forwards twirling a white handkerchief in my hand. My performance was superb; but it continued always to be very vivid, very much underscored.

Sir, you began not with heavily marked passages; you began with no disproportionate accentuation, but with an outline already finished, distributed, even. From the moment the curtain rose on you sitting there, the picture of pale thought and brooding, dear loss, to the end, when you were carried by death and the strong arms of action up that flight of stairs and out beyond that high arch, you made of your idea one unbroken and complete line.

But one thinks not so much of any particular business of yours or any one scene, as of a distinguished continuity and taste. What you will have to do, then, Sir, reverses my necessity. You will have to fill in your design.

Sir, I erred—as I see now—and you err, in making this character and life of Hamlet too simple. Neither of us would admit it whole. My age, which was the age of Dr. Johnson and Sir Joshua Reynolds, followed close on the heels of an age of reason, of Mr. Pope and Mr. Addison, and the social philosophy of the French. To us Shakespeare's creation seemed a little barbaric, confused. And the graveyard scene seemed a vulgar muddle; I used to refer, indeed, to the rubbish of the fifth act. I cut that scene, left out the grave-diggers entirely. I altered the scenes with Ophelia and wrote in lines to make them more intelligible. I made the aspect of the character elegantly familiar, dressing Hamlet in the French fashion of the time, the black coat,

knee breeches, the waistcoat with flaps; I wore
my own hair. In sum, though I left the whole
of it aristocratic and fine, I reduced Shakespeare's play to the thought of my century.
You, Sir, have erred toward your democratic
epoch. You simplify the play overmuch by
making Hamlet too easy to understand; by putting him in terms too satisfactory to your public.

A part of your success is due to your presence
and magnetism and to your capital achievements in playing. But a part of it also is due to
your making Hamlet very easy to digest. Your
audience of free democratic citizens feel that,
for the first time, they understand what it all
means. But, Sir, Hamlet is the dreamer, the
human soul beating itself out against limitations, the scholar, prince, lover, wit, poet,
clown, the mystery. And so he remains not real
but, as it were, super-real. I see now that the
very essence of Hamlet is that we could never
understand him.

In your scenes with Polonius you were admirable. Most actors for the applause they get
play up for all it is worth Hamlet's rude wit at

the old man's expense. But you gave us only Hamlet's sense of the world grown empty and life turned to rubbish in this old counselor and Hamlet's sense that in Polonius was represented that special element in life that had robbed him of Ophelia.

Your many economies, Sir, were superb. The nunnery scene with Ophelia was done with a reaching out of hands almost; in the closet scene the relation of Hamlet to his mother and through her to the ghost was achieved by his moving toward the ghost on his knees and being caught in his mother's arms, weaving together the bodies of those two, who, whatever their sins might be, must belong to each other at such terrible cost. About your performance there were none of those accessories in invented stage business, but only that action proceeding from the inner necessity and leaning on the play's life, not on stage expedients. But if you would carry forward from this first performance in the year 1922 the poetry and mystery of Hamlet, you must create the sense of a larger inner tumult, and indeed of a certain cerebral and passionate ecstasy, pressing against the external restraint of him. Your Hamlet needs the suggestion of more vitality, ungovernable and deep, of more complex suffering, of not only intellectual subtlety but intellectual power as well, of the shy and humourous mystery, the proud irony, the storms of pain. With your fine, clear outline give Hamlet the nuance of more shadow, more of a fitful magnificence, more confusion, more inexplicability. And, most of all, you must give to your creation more poetry and richness of soul; there is lacking in your art a fulness, a kind of noble generosity, to make it spacious and profound.

Sir, the whole theory of an art of acting that the Europe of my day held, was not that which obtains in your generation. Under that theory acting was fundamentally a separable thing from the actor's state of feeling. Technique in itself was highly considered; sheer mentality played a conspicuous part in an actor's effects and the audience's pleasure. The test of an actor lay in his possession of a general talent, the ability to do all rôles with an equal truth. Toward this versatility the equipment of an actor consisted, first of all, of mimetic powers and of a face and figure capable of every variety of expression. And finally he required an intelligence that could build up out of reality an idea to be created.

For such an art I had every gift. In my first season I astounded London by acting with the same success Richard III, a rascally valet, a uxorious Puritan, a fop, a conceited author, and then in one evening King Lear and Master Johnny, a country lout. My mimetic gifts, my eyes, nose, mouth and voice, were such that I could pass through many characters and emotions in a few minutes, completely different in each. In the salons of Paris, where I was adored, I acted the dagger scene from Macbeth with overwhelming and tragic beauty, and passed from that into a cook's boy letting fall a tray of pies into the gutter. My body was in perfect proportion, and I seemed to be present in every muscle. My very presence on the stage had an air of life. I was, of all things, first an actor.

To your ears and your public such details of physique and technical means sound merely external. Certes, if left so, they would be. But, Sir, never believe that I went no further. I knew the uses of these resources. I knew that the actor must have his idea and his effects prepared and ready. But I knew also that

great acting could never stop there. I knew
that from genius there must be the life blood
that bursts forth and, like a flame, shoots
through the spectators' veins. I knew that in
the greatest moments in acting, the actor has
the feeling of the instant come upon him un-
expectedly. I testified that the greatest strokes
of genius have been unknown to the actor himself till circumstances and the warmth of the
scene have sprung the mine, as it were, as much
to his surprise as to that of the audience. This
I made the difference between great genius and
good playing: good players give pleasure by
their strong power and good sense; the great
genius will always realize the feelings of the
character and be transported beyond himself.
It is this great and generous translation beyond
yourself that you will most need.

Sir, your art, and the theory of art that your
age maintains, are more private than mine,
less social and general and separable from the
personality of the actor. You have not so
many of these external acting gifts as I had.
You have an admirable presence, but you are
not mimetic; your pantomime could mean little
in itself. Your body and your face are not

eminently flexible and expressive. Your features are incisive, delicate, significant, rather than mobile. Your voice is admirable, but not yet a great instrument; it is still something conscious of its training. Your delivery of the verse is good but lacks somewhat that resistant flexibility, to use an old phrase, that is the soul of fine reading. You of all things are first not the actor but the artist, yet you attain to beautiful acting. At your best, for your performances vary in excellence from night to night, you excel in what a painter might call the fine drawing of your scenes, in the outward simplicity of your method, and your power to create on the stage not so much the action of a drama as the air of a compelling mood. But the fundamental principles of your art and mine remain the same. Your business, as mine was, is to labor toward finding in your art a language suited to the finest reaches of your time.

MOLLY NELSON TO MARGALO
GILLMORE

My dear Young Lady: I was an actress whose name you have never heard and nobody among your friends ever heard of me. I was born in Louisiana, in the seventies, in a village not far from New Orleans, of a Scotch father and a French mother. When I was twelve years old a company of actors came to our town for a fortnight, playing *Richelieu* and *Romeo and Juliet* and a number of old-fashioned farces and melodramas. My mother and I went to see them one night, then the next night we returned and took my father. My father and mother after that, though they had enjoyed the play, would have stayed at home, for they were moderate and thrifty people; but I would go again; I cried all night; and they, to humor me, for I was an only child, took me again; and so it came about that every night I went to see that company of actors.

From that day I meant to be an actress. I said so to my parents and they laughed at me. They had already other hopes for me, my father toward my education and establishment in life, my mother toward marriage and a family. When I was older I spoke of it again; my mother wept, my father, who was a religious Scotchman and a tyrant, threatened, if I persisted, to turn me on the streets. At seventeen I considered myself a woman and announced my intention to run away, if I must, and join a company playing in New Orleans; and my father ordered me out of his house and sent my things after me. I never saw either of my parents again.

In New Orleans I found at last a chance to become an actress. My beauty and my eagerness made a way for me. The company I joined played sometimes in the city, but for the most part went barnstorming through the country, through Louisiana and lower Mississippi and into Alabama. The actors in it were mostly poor, stupid people without talent or ambition, a few of them through drink or bad fortune had come down in the world from better theatres. My success with my audiences was so great that almost from the very first I was given leading parts. I acted oftenest in the worthless plays of the day, which in the provinces were

low indeed; for sometimes our company served
not only as entertainment but as an advertise-
ment for a patent liniment. In our travels to
and from the towns we put up signs along the
roadside, telling how our remedy cured sprains
and rheumatism. In one play my old father
was killed by a villain and I, dressed in a long
green velvet gown, was obliged to end my great
scene by saying: "Here, over the dead body of
my father, I, Jean Ingleside, do swear to have
my revenge." But the part I loved best was
Juliet, which because of my beauty and romantic youth we played now and then. Even in
the most miserable of these Southern places
there was some faint glamour around high-
sounding names like Shakespeare's.

Meantime I studied continuously, there were
plenty of books from the city; I kept to myself
as much as I could, learning part after part,
dreaming of finding my way to New York, of
becoming a great actress and some day speaking to the world. But years passed, there was
nobody to carry me out of the round that had
caught me. I had only a country fame for my
reward. And one night, long before I was
thirty, I died of pneumonia, which I had caught

going fifty feet through a snow-storm up an outside stair from my dressing-room to the stage in the hall where we were playing.

Dear young lady, I saw you in Andreyev's *He Who Gets Slapped*. In this play the part of Consuelo, the bareback rider, fell to you. She is young, simple, free, innocent, driven by her foster father to the arms of the fat baron; drawn, dimly, to Bezano, her partner in the circus. She is perplexed when He speaks, the philosopher who, when he had grown sick with the mediocrity and treachery of the world of men, has come to the circus to be the clown that gets slapped; and in the end she dies poisoned by him to save her from her fate. Dear young lady, you played Consuelo very prettily. You were dainty and innocent and fair; I watched you enter, and laugh, and listen when He spoke his wonderful lines about the goddess rising from the sea foam; I watched your terror of the disgusting fat suitor, your shy looking after Bezano. It was a very pretty little princess in a fairy tale that you played.

But what a part that was you had! Could you not see what this girl was? The baron seeks her for a beastly purpose because he is a beast. Bezano seeks her as the woman for him; the circus people love her as the favored child among them; He, the clown, loves her because she is like his own dream. And Consuelo herself is the centre of the play, which turns on the theme of love. She is the thing itself, unconscious of what she is. She is all beauty, untouched by the world, complete in itself, seen only at moments, perfect, immortal. She should have been there on the stage the thing within life that all life seeks and that shines through all as a light shining through a restless and passionate dream.

Dear young lady, I worked. I used constantly to watch people's faces on the street and when they listened to music. And when I played in New Orleans I used to slip away sometimes all day and wander on the outskirts of the town till I came to the great cemetery of St. Roch. I used to wander in those avenues of vaults and under the dark pines and magnolias and through the box walks. There were many statues in the place, marble saints, images of Christ and his mother, angels and ideal figures of the dead. I used to walk about looking at these statues, stopping as if to visit them. I tried to imagine what they were thinking in such a long silence as they kept. Some of them I loved; and I tried to imitate their gestures. I tried to pour through my body the lines of a statue and, standing before it, to make my limbs, my head and arms and legs, alive with the same life as the life in it. I sought to gain for my body the unforgettable images that these marbles caught. When we were in smaller towns I used to escape to the country and walk hours, mad, lost in my dream, till twilight came down over the fields and over the water of the pools and I was obliged at last to hurry back to the theatre.

And then that night on the stage the thought of the country lying tranquil in the night air or of those marble figures standing there bowed or holding up their arms in the starlight, came over me and seemed the meaning of the eternal life beneath all art; and I could not go on; I stood speechless; and in that pause of silence I could feel a thrill run through my audience, and a moment later a thunder of applause came. What would I have given to have played this Consuelo! And to have played it before an audience of New York, or of any of the great capitals of the world!

Dear young lady, I think of you in that rôle of Consuelo that fortune sent you, and of your prosperity in the theatre. And with you I think of other young actresses in New York whom luck has visited and who have taken so pleasantly these wonderful parts that fell to them. There is, for one example, Ruth Chatterton, who had Mary Rose to play. Barrie's piece is loose, is foolish in places and sentimental. But what a part Mary Rose would be, the girl, the dream in two worlds, called away by the spirits, drawn back years later to her son—the ghost of love, the eternal mystery! Or, among others, Jeanne de Casalis, who went so mildly through the part of Violaine in Claudel's *L'Annonce Fait à Marie*, when there was in it the gamut of love, pain and our endurance of every-day plain things and the sacrament of life and death and birth. What fortunate stars gave you young actresses these parts!

But I, who dreamed so and gave myself so to life, never had a chance. Nobody ever saw me who could do anything to bring me to good fortune. My audiences loved me more than they did my fellow actors because I was so real and shining and intense; but they took me without thought, merely for what I gave them, as they took the sun, the moon, human love, the coming of spring in the world around them. And, for all the world of men and art ever knew, I was no more than any of these things in nature that are so taken for granted, and so I died as a chance love ends or the spring or summer passes, I who might have been, if any opportunity had ever allowed, a great artist. And so fortune in art favors some, and some are left to waste and drop out, unknown, lost, unarrived anywhere.

MLLE. BEAUVAL TO A TEA-PARTY AT THE RITZ

MESDEMOISELLES and Messieurs, I came to your tea, climbing down from Paradise not many more stairs than I had when I came from my attic in the rue St. Louis every night to go to the theatre. I saw at your party a charming company. There were ladies and there were gentlemen, every one charmingly, though somewhat expectedly, dressed. Some of you, no matter from where you came first to New York, appeared to be of a society truly urban; some were a little more like the provinces touched off with urban vulgarities.

Still it was an agreeable scene, such comfort and well-being and competitive complaisance, more chic than the angels I had left, but no less easy and secure from want. The apartment was warm as June in Avignon when we played there in the bishop's garden, though from your wide windows at the Ritz the snow and ice crackled outside over the roofs of New York. And how adorable were the flowers; their odors mingled

with the ladies' perfumes from my dear Paris!
And near by, through the tall door, was the glittering bath with its seas of hot and cold water,
its porcelain and tiles and acres of towels; the
Pompadour herself had nothing like it. And
what chairs and lounges!

And to all this, to this room, with the summer
there, and the flowers and cushions, rose the elevator in the hallway outside, sweeping your
bodies upward from the earth as only, in my
time, the souls of men, however great they
were, could rise. It was not like my stair.

Meantime the conversation went on, newspapers, automobiles, Newport and many springs,
trips to Europe—you all go to Europe or at
least to Paris, is it not so?—clothes, gossip of the
theatre, just the right breath of scandal, too, for
the drawing-room, and a few whispered gutter
dregs, and something now and then about the
new players and the companies from abroad. I
looked from one lady to another, one gentleman
to another gentleman, and listened to what you
said, finding it all most pleasant, I assure you.

But what troubled me, dear Mesdemoiselles
and Messieurs, was this: I could not tell the
artists from the others. I looked at the gentle-

men without result. I looked at the ladies.
Which were artists and which were not? I had
thought there might be some look perhaps,
something in the eye, some record of intensity,
of pain, or joy or courage. Or there might be
some exactitude of the features, or some bearing
to go by. You, Messieurs, were all manly and
agreeable, good traits for all men. And you,
Mesdemoiselles, whether actresses or not, were
one only more delightful than another. The
difficulty was, Mesdemoiselles, I had never
known that the end of art was to approximate
a lady.

But then, how should I know this: I was never
received into the society of my day in France.
Before I came to Paris to join the King's company I was in the provinces. I was the adopted
daughter of Filandre, the manager of our company—only adopted by Filandre, I was actually
the cast-off child of some Dutchman.

You know what happened to us, you have
read all that in M. Scarron's *Roman Comique*.
We used to bump around in carts from town to
town, acting in tennis-courts, in rich lords' halls,
in hostelries and on the bridges. Some of us were
good artists, some were bad. There was, for ex-

ample, little, dark La Racune, who if he had been good to drink, would have filled hardly two glasses, and so bad an actor that if there were police to preserve the laws of the theatre he would have been arrested nightly. On the other hand, there was the divine Louis, who, though he rode on a donkey, could spout as he went the verses of Théophile's tragedy with such style that the peasants we passed took off their caps and crossed themselves.

You may have read how we came into the town of Mans once with a cart laden with trunks and packs of painted cloths that made a pyramid on which I sat, drawn by a pair of lean oxen and a breeding mare, whose colt ran alongside. Destin walked beside me, as poor in habit as rich in mien, a patch over one eye and half one cheek, and with a string at his belt of crows, magpies, hens, and geese, like the spoils of war. And Rancour came behind, carrying a bass viol on his back and looking like a great tortoise walking on its hind legs. There were only these of us, the rest of the company was fled to Alençon from Tours, where our door-keeper had killed a soldier. Nevertheless in **half an hour** we were giving a play, Destin lying on a quilt and saying Herod's lines, and I playing Salome.

A fight in the audience prevented the finish of the play, it is true; but we recited grandly; even now in Paradise sometimes the lines ring in my ears. At that time I had a husband in the troupe, for I became enamored of Jean Pitel, our candle snuffer, and I dare say I married him. At any rate, time passed and all things happened. All dangers, every sort of glory. We played everywhere, inns, palaces, tennis-courts. We were cold, hot, hungry, rich, poor, in fortune and out. Ruffians captured our young women, barons and great ladies loved us, we found once a dead man under the bed. But we learned our craft.

At any rate, one fine day came the order from St. Germain. *De par le Roi!* His Majesty wishing always to keep the troupe of his comedians complete and to that end taking the best from the provinces, and being informed that the said Beauval— In sum, I went to the Palais Royal and Molière's company. I took up my abode under the roof there in the rue St. Louis. What triumphs were mine! And then the Duke took me up, and there was luxury. But though

I lived richly and my art went on to greater triumphs, I still belonged to a world made up only of artists and gay adventurers and wild, brave nobles who went their own ways. I was only a player, and so I lived my life. I knew no ladies and I went to no great house. I never dreamed once of being a lady, though it is true I did dream of becoming a great artist.

But nowadays, Mesdemoiselles and Messieurs, it is so charmingly different, is it not? I do not see them among your company at tea, but there are no doubt artists who are less blest, less about town, more bitten and hurt, more set on learning a great craft. You will not need that craft. You may not know much, but you know a great many people and almost anybody might be you. I must be happy in seeing you on the stage as you are off it and seeing you do there what you do everywhere. Some of you had your torments and ambitions once, I dare say, but you grew quickly up into the general, and found in time your reassurance in success. It may be some one else's kind of success rather than one's own kind, but, even at that, success in the land of Success is a great balm.

You come to the theatre. Your public have had a busy day going in and out of places and keeping as much like one another as they can. They have been gathering their ideas from the newspapers and journals, where you get yours. They never hiss, they applaud with willing energy. You may well delight in pleasing them. Let the foreigners, if they choose, abandon themselves to theatrical outbursts and lose their good practical sense, but not you. Sometimes they too, if the seasons favor them, learn to play the game and get their interesting faces to look more sensible and vacant.

Hotel and country club and parlor car æsthetics and you, its obliging artists, more alike than even the photographers and hairdressers can turn you—the public that is yours is able to make itself at home in art. The gutter has its violence and its release from tense and cramped reserves; there are the schools of poverty, one-night stands, reckless aspiration, loneliness; there is the long labor by which a craft is got. The people in vaudeville and in circuses must reach some edge of vivid life; but I can look you over as cheerily as one does the mildly artistic, mildly lustful, and pretty covers on your news-stands. In my day actors were not received in society. In the eyes of society we remained instruments for which it was not responsible but in which it saw expressed and enlivened the beauty and powers and desires of life. I can easily imagine myself understudying, as I did once in fact, Mlle. de Brie or even Béjart, but I should find it hard to understudy the department stores, clubs, teas, and social receptions. Mesdemoiselles and Messieurs, it is for an actor very often that a dramatist writes his play. Doubtless, some one here at your tea is writing plays that are fitted nicely to your quality. He knows exactly how far to go, what to put into his plays, and so all prosper together.

Yet you may be right, with your salaries, your apartments and suppers, your motors, cabs, social engagements, your gowns from the splendid windows, your good long runs and easy manners. In such a state of affairs an artist is free. He may do as any one does. And if your public would have you thus, who can blame you? If you express what they want expressed, what else is there to say, save that you are fortunate indeed in being able as artists to arrive at your summits in terms so simple as these? And meantime people applaud, and set one against another your interesting personalities, and strive to meet you and invite you everywhere. In a fashion, of course, it is flattering for them that artists should be so like themselves.

THE ART OF DIRECTING

THE ART OF DIRECTING

IN the course of stage history the director
has borne a varied name and a more varied relationship to the theatre. He has sometimes
been the owner of the play, sometimes an actor
from the company, sometimes the régisseur,
or director of the entire production in all its
parts, sometimes the producer or actor-manager.
But whatever the problem of the régisseur, or
producer, or actor-manager may be elsewhere,
in our American theatre at present the director
is the man with the script in his hand who
stands behind the whole performance of the
play, who, to varying degrees, prescribes what
the interpretation shall be, what the actors
shall do, and trains them how to do it. He is
the *maestro*, the coach, the general behind the
rehearsals.

The director is the artist who takes the drama
as it is put into his hands and labors to re-
create it in his own technical terms. And this

[157]

drama, when it is re-created into these terms, becomes theatre and something that is different from what it was before. Directing is an art or it is nothing.

There is no such thing as a play directed exactly as it is written any more than there is a landscape painted as it really is. In any art the material that goes to make up the work suffers a change before it becomes this work, and this change, this something added, derives from the artist working. In Corot's Ville d'Avray the material was the landscape of trees, atmosphere, and light; the medium was the paint. In Houdon's Voltaire the material was a body and the character in that body; the medium the marble. The dramatist's material is men, life, experience; his medium the dramatic form. In the art of the director the drama itself is the material, and the actor in the midst of the audience and the designer's décor is his medium. It follows that when a drama emerges from the hands of the director it has undergone a restatement of itself, a translation into the terms of the theatre, and the importance of the thing added will measure the importance of the director.

THE ART OF DIRECTING

Most directors are not distinctly one type or another; they belong in the middle ground between two extremes. But at one extreme in directing is the virtuoso. He takes the play into his own hands and does with it what he chooses, twists it, makes it his own. He may go the limit in violating its quality, in forcing it to his own ends.

At the other extreme is the director whose aim is to carry out entirely the dramatist's idea. If the play is bombastic he makes his rendering of it bombastic, where it is cold he will be cold, where it is barren he keeps it barren, and so on; he covers nothing, he tries to discover and to restate in theatre terms the play's essential character and the style that expresses this character; to every element in the play he means to give its special quality and intention.

Both these types of directors are artists. If one appears more sharply than the other to be an artist, it is not because of his method, but because what he creates is better or worse. It is a difference in degree, not in kind. We may prefer a performer who tries to play a concerto as closely as he can to what is written rather than one who sweeps it out of itself to his own mood and will. But in the end what finally decides the question as to whether or not either of the performers is an artist is the thing created. With Liszt, Schubert may become not only the material that Liszt interprets but also the material from which he creates something violently his own. The virtuoso director at his peril does what he wills in directing a play. He may be a good artist or a bad, according to the result that he creates, but he is an artist. The result must judge itself. The original drama may almost disappear before such a director has done with it, but, conceivably at least, we may be willing to forget it quite in order to possess the new creation, as we are willing to forget in El Greco the likeness of trees in order to achieve El Greco. In the theatre the trouble, however, with the virtuoso lies in the fact that there will always be few directors who have as much to give us as have the plays that they direct.

Great talents like Gordon Craig may do what they like with a play, and risk the outcome. Gordon Craig might take *Othello*, for example, and change it into what, as a whole, it but slightly could be, or read into it something that it scarcely contains at all, and yet create for us a result magnificent in itself. Or he might lift one element in the play to an importance out of all proportion to the whole of it, and by doing so illumine and dilate forever the region that *Othello* can express. A dozen Gordon Craigs bringing to bear on Shakespeare's tragedy this radiant distortion and dilation in twelve different aspects might increase twelve times *Othello's* radiance and scope. But Gordon Craigs are rare. And we are apt to feel that any one so determined to say what he has to say rather than what the dramatist intended, should let the play alone and write another for himself.

The kind of director at the other extreme from the virtuoso would by some persons be rejected entirely as a creative artist—to use a phrase that is often heard but that makes no sense, since an artist is an artist only in so far as he is creative. To reply to that we may best set aside the comparison between the director and the play he uses and El Greco and the trees

that go into his painting of a landscape. Shall
we say an orchestra leader and his rendering
of a Beethoven Symphony, and a director and
the play that he presents? In this case what
comes to the artist is already established; as
was not the case with the landscape, something
is already created. The score is ready to his
hand. Into it the artist, working in his own
terms, strives to create life and thus to express
it. But if every instrument in the orchestra
rendered exactly the score written for it we
should still not have the symphony created.
Not in nature, ideas, or art is there any truth
that is ready and expressed and the same; it
is restated in every man that experiences it
and as significantly as the observer is significant.
No director can give us a play as it is, however
faithful his intention may be and however
great his ability to carry out his intention. His
ideal may be a fine one; he strives to disappear
and to leave the play exposed and expressed,
to achieve a style that is an invisible medium,
like a laboratory glass that reveals the delicate
processes of an experiment. But he remains
the artist by whose creation this style and
revelation may arrive.

THE ART OF DIRECTING

The relation among a play's ideas, remarks, events, and emotions, how they follow one another, how they dispose themselves together and so reveal the whole meaning of the play, is expressed, in so far as concerns their precise meanings and definite points, through words and actions. The exact observations that Hamlet has to make on his own failure in the power to act is expressed when he says:

"Why, what an ass am I ! This is most brave
That I, the son of a dear father murdered,
Prompted to my revenge by heaven and hell,
Must, like a whore, unpack my heart with words,
And fall a-cursing like a very drab,
A scullion !"

When we see Pirandello's hero daub paint on his face and put on the robes of Henry at Canossa, we know exactly what theme and disguise his plan has followed.

But these are more special and particularized elements of a drama. Beneath them lies the main body of the play. In the whole of it there is the emphasis of one part compared with another; the mass is stressed heavily here and lightly there, according to its importance in the whole. One speech leaps out from another, propelled by the inner conflict beneath them. One speech is distant from those near it because it arises from meditation in the speaker or from his continuous habit of thought. One speech is ready in the speaker's heart before the thing it seems to answer has been said, its lips were on the other's lips ere they were born. The pulse or beat of a line or a speech or a scene is here quick, there slow; the emotion or thought exhilarates, it retards. All these are a matter of pure relationships. Beneath the particular situation, the particular thoughts, reactions, deeds, every play can be reduced to this abstract basis. Every play has this abstract pattern of values. On this side it is for the most part closely connected with the art of music. A director can best study the layout of a play as if it were a musical composition.

Music, as every one knows, is of all arts, except architecture perhaps, the most ideal. That is to say, music does not involve imitation or concrete instance or definite concept; its region is pure to itself. Music is the beautiful eternity, the idea, the essence, the general quality. In sum, to take an example, where Hamlet can only say to us,

"I have that within which passeth show,"

music can put us into the very state itself out of which this poetry or our tears arise. But this, of course, is a commonplace about the art.

In the play the matter of emphasis, themes and characters and events, the speed, the vocal tone, rest all fundamentally and essentially on a base of music. The relation of the stream of points equidistant from one point is a part of the truth of a circle, an abstract thing. The height of a tower is a part of its idea. The quiet of the vowels and the contemplative measure in one of Virgil's pastoral verses is as much its truth as is the precise thing said in words, and to forget this is to forget the nature of art. To forget this is like saying that a madness to kill is expressed or conveyed in a remark stating, "I am going to kill you," rather than in the eye and the onward rush of the murderer. The length, the beat, the duration of a speech in a play are a part of its idea. The time between two speeches is a part of their meaning. The tempo at which a cue is taken and the tone of the voice

[165]

are as much—and often far more so—the truth
of a speech as the more exact and limiting words
that are said. When Othello says:

"Never, Iago. Like to the Pontic Sea,
   Whose icy current and compulsive course
   Ne'er keeps retiring ebb, but keeps due on
   To the Propontic and the Hellespont;
   Even so my bloody thoughts, with violent pace
   Shall ne'er look back, ne'er ebb to humble love,
   Till that a capable and wide revenge
   Swallow them up——"

the main truth of the outburst, the sheer fact
that it is an outburst even, is conveyed by a tremendous current in the declamation, by the vocal tone and flood of sound rather than by the
special concept in each and every phrase. And
unless this outline and rhythm are established,
the speech breaks down into something of
forced images and elaborate if not false details.

When Marchbanks, with the poet's insight,
says to Prossy of the arid, hot heart and bitter,
drab profession, that he can see nothing in
Morell but words, pious resolutions, and asks if
it is possible for a woman to love him, and Prossy, after trying to evade the question, says,
   "Yes,"
it is obvious that except for her mere acknowl-

edgment of a fact, the whole moving truth must lie in the time she takes before she speaks and in the tone of her voice. When Miss Clare Eames acted the part it was almost wholly her musical sense that made this particular moment in the play so mordant and touching. The Hopkins production of *The Deluge*, very interesting in its intention, wore out long before the end, because in this situation, where a group of people, shut in by the flood and faced with death, show reformations and candid fires not usual with them, and later, when safety comes, revert to their daily selves, the more or less dramatic repetition in the scenes depended for its point on a variation in tempo which was not achieved. And, finally, in the case of individual actors it is their time sense, their sense of the exact moment for a cue, a speech, an answer, that does as much as anything else to engage the audience's attention with its constantly fresh vitality and surprise.

VISUAL MUSIC

There is an element, of course, in the performance of a play that speaks entirely to our eyes. When the director begins to consider the expression of this aspect of a play he may wisely study every part of it as a set of pure relationships, a kind of visual music. He can study as he might a symphony what is the essential idea of a play and what groups, motions, positions will most help in expressing through the eye what the other dramatic mediums are expressing through our other faculties or channels of perception. He can define those lines and masses on the stage, and then subordinate what is secondary and omit some of the confusion of empty or extraneous movements. He can study a scene for its last, fundamental idea or characteristic and try to find what line, what visual quality, will most express the essential idea of the scene; and can employ that line as something in itself expressive. And he can seek to establish what is most important of all these, the visual continuity of the scene, its living rhythm in our eyes, from the time it begins till it ends.

THE DIRECTOR'S MEDIUM

Granted a clear or important idea for the play that he will present and the means and ability to carry it through, the director has still a problem like that of any artist, who for the prosperity of a work has to consider what tact and judgment he will use to achieve the right relationship between the work and the public. There is a point beyond which if an artist carries his idea he will lose the sympathy of his public and so defeat his own end, which is to express his idea to them. On the other hand, too much consideration of his public may prevent the artist's going far enough to reach the point at which his idea will get itself expressed. In every art some concession, obviously, is unescapable; music, for instance, has to be loud enough to be audible; the musician must concede that much at least to his public. But in general as an artist you may choose to trim your sails in order to arrive at your wished-for port, or you may choose to miss the temporary destination or success and instead to stretch the bounds of your art, to chart new seas, to sight new forms, new possibilities for expression. You take your choice at your peril and according to your own nature.

But the artist directing in the theatre has to remember that the theatre essentially is an impure medium. It consists not only of what is on the stage but of the audience in front.

The director will have to make an imaginative choice and proportionment of parts, so as not to leave out the audience from his creation. However prophetic or illuminating the stage end of his creation may be, if the audience is not rightly involved in it the creation suffers, as might be the case with a pianist who insisted on pouring water into the instrument for the sake of some future aquatic scale, but failed of any sound or anything besides his strong idea or inspiration. The director has to consider what effect he most seeks, what is the truth that he would most express. When this is found he must relate every detail to it, taking his choice as to how far he is creating for a complete present moment and how far for future innovation or extension. A thing admirably right in itself may, when the audience sees it, jump out of the frame and distort the whole picture. An unwelcome detail, however true in itself, may either wreck the truth of a whole scene or send it to a thrilling pitch. To say what has never been allowed said on the stage, what has been more or less banned as crass or outrageous, may swamp the play or may double its expressiveness. The director may take whatever chance he likes, but he has to work in all the elements of his art—the play, the actors, the audience.

RESTATEMENTS OF PLAYS

When a play is new, hot from the author's forge, it may be taken as written for its own time, its idea is stated for the dramatist's own generation. The director's business is an interpretation of it in theatrical terms. But when there is a play to be revived, a few years or some centuries from its birth, the director's problem takes on another shift in restatement.

In so far as a play was ever a work of art it was a living thing. Within his dramatic form the dramatist has arrested and found a right body for a section in the stream of life. Life may be said to rise and to fill for a moment such a form. But the very essence of life as distinguished from the dead is this streaming, this ever-changing current of it. The living content, no longer wholly arrested in this form, goes on with its stream and is not to be distinguished from it. The form without the content is empty and dead. In the history of an art the process toward degeneration, and through and past that to a new summit of excellence, a new epoch, consists of two courses: First, there is the survival of the form with less and less of the sustaining life that once brought the form into being; this is the so-called decadence of an art. Second, there is the progress of a new quality of life needing its body and moving toward a form that will contain and express it.

In Euripides's *Bacchæ* Dionysos, the god of ever-springing life and enthusiasm and ecstasy, could not be bound; prison-bars, fetters, no obstacle had power to hold him fast. Only the forms of his own passion and of his own thought and his own motion could contain his divine life.

Pirandello, for the modern theatre, has dramatized this idea. The theme in Pirandello's work is the dualism between Life on one hand and Form on the other; on the one hand Life pouring in a stream, unknowable, obscure, unceasing; on the other hand forms, ideas, crystallizations, in which we try to embody and express this ceaseless stream of Life. Upon everything lies the burden of its form, which alone separates it from dust, but which also interferes with the unceasing flood of Life in it.

In *Henry IV* this man who has taken on Form, a fixed mask in the midst of changing Life, remains in it until the moment when his passion and despair and violent impulse send him back into Life. But only for a moment; the impetuous violence of the Life in him expels him into his masquerade again; in his tragic struggle between Life and Form, Life is defeated, Form remains.

To many a play, when it is revived, comes such a fate as this. The life in the play is defeated, the ironic form remains.

The performance of a play at the director's hands is not a mere matter of the written text. Its truth can arise only from the combination of this text as it stands, plus the audience for whom it is given. In so far as a play is alive the living element in it is an impalpable, on-running, delicately perilous reality on which an illusion of permanence has been imposed by its form. The life in *Macbeth*, for example, seems to be permanently expressed by the play as we read it, and this might seem to hold true even for its performance. But this, in fact, is not the case. In such a performance there might be academic phases of interest. As history of literature, as drama, as Shakespearian tragedy, it might, if you choose, possess an interest. But such kinds of interest, though studious and engaging, are apart from the play's vitality as art. And this is just the point at which we need most the director's imagination, need the genius in him for re-creating the play in the necessary new terms.

That side of Shakespeare's *Macbeth* that is a living thing, that speaks to the life in us and arouses a response from it, and fecundates and increases the volume of that life, must be restated in every revival—and in a sense, indeed, at every performance—of the play. The life in this play is not a fact, it is not a fixed and permanent statement; it is an ever-changing reality, unconfinable, a ceaseless flux, but real. The sixteenth-century *Macbeth* of Shakespeare derives from an earlier and more primitive base. It has beneath it such an element of shock and terror as is to be found nowhere else in drama. This primitive quality Shakespeare restated in terms of the morality and the complex style of his own Elizabethan age, and lo, we have his *Tragedy of Macbeth*. And now, in turn, this primitive quality and this Elizabethanness must be restated for us. Even if a director could discover every fact, every piece of business, exact reading, gesture, tone, of the first production of *Macbeth*, and could reproduce them for us to the last jot, he would not necessarily convey to us the life in the play. He might give us only something beautifully curious or antiquarian or historic, exhibitions in facsimile, but not *Macbeth* and its meaning to us. No, his business as an artist is to discover a rendering for *Macbeth*—which is his material—through his medium—which is first the actors and the décor of his theatre —to discover a rendering of such a kind as will restate for the audience present the significance of the life of the play. There is no right way to produce *Macbeth*. It would be a comfort to think so, to have something to rest upon, just as some right way of living would be a comfort. But with life and with art the same thing holds: the essence of being alive is a constant, perilous choice and a constant projection of imagination into living forms.

A part of the truth of a Greek play is its distance from us in time. To be alive it has to be restated for us somewhat as its original mate-

rial had to be restated in it. For us a part of
a Greek play's truth is its Greekness, with all
that that may mean for us. In Restoration
times a gentleman often carried a little bowl of
gold or silver which he could take from his
pocket and rest on the arm of his chair, and
into it from time to time might spit. Molière's
gallants did a smart thing when they took a
comb from their pockets and arranged their
curls as they sat in a lady's salon. But the director who wished to give us the quality of
gallant gentlemen in his revival of these social
comedies could not show us such details, they
would defeat his ends and give us not elegance
but only ugliness. These are simple instances,
but they illustrate the case. What in these
particular instances needs most to be conveyed
is the living thing, the permanent idea in them
to which we respond—in sum, their elegance.
At whatever cost, this must be created or the
moment is empty.

The director's revival of a play, then, is a
form of creation, and in so far as this is not so
the play lies dead on the stage, a mere fact, the
empty shell where once there was an engaging
life. All compromise, change, or emphasis in a

new production of an old play can have but this one end, which is in a way to keep it alive. The extent to which the director preserves closely the play in its original shape, or violates or distorts it, re-creates its essentials in new terms or even forces it so that we hardly recognize it for the same play, may affect the success of his enterprise, but it does not alter the principle involved. There are as many ways of doing *Macbeth* as there are generations of human life; and in its production the perpetual creation of a right body to express its truth is the condition on which alone *Macbeth* is kept not merely a matter of culture but a thing that is alive in our experience.

USE OF THE ACTOR

When the director, as an orchestra leader might, has achieved through the actors under him the desired emphasis throughout the performance, the time values, the tone, and so on, he remains to be considered as any artist in general making use of the means at hand. We may think of him as an artist in the use of his medium.

Of late years there has arisen in the theatre

a type of directing that proceeds on the basis of letting the actor alone. Up to the point of collision with the other players the actor can go his own way and almost unmolested in creating his rôle. The principle is to get good actors and let them go ahead. Up to a certain point this policy has worked. But it has been a limited and often fatal method. Provided you get good actors, and in cases where only one or two actors carry the whole burden of the scene and can, perhaps, work it out between the two of them, you may succeed. But in general the scheme is almost as hopeless as turning a crew of sailors loose without an officer to run the ship. And, moreover, this method leads to a relaxation and laziness in the director himself.

The other extreme in directing actors is an older and more tried policy. In it the one hand controls everything and every one involved in the play, and not only controls the actor but dominates his conception of a rôle and the entire playing of it. Such a director at such an extreme may even give the actor the tone, the gesture, the movement. He may, when he likes, make the actor an imitation of himself. Up to a certain point this method also has often worked. If we must choose, it is on the whole safer than the opposite extreme. Provided the director himself has ideas that are capable of making the play into something worth while, and has the force or control to work the actors into his will, he may succeed. And the discouraging inferiority of the mass of actors seems to argue for such a tyranny. But it obviously throws away no little of the individual resonance of the actor. And it tends to mechanize actors and to make them stale. It gives them stage tricks where real invention is needed; it leads them toward a more or less passive exploitation of themselves.

The necessity of the second method, the one controlling head for the performance, is plain. The whole scale of the play finally depends on that. The good element in the first method, the hands-off-and-let-the-actor-do-it school of directing, consists in the fact that at its best it allows the actor freedom to create and the possibility of succeeding in himself, of happiness in his own soul. It leads him toward becoming a better and better medium in which the director may work. The ideal directing combines the two methods.

But of the actor as medium there is more to say. As the medium in which the director works, the actor may be thought of somewhat as paint is thought of for the painter or marble for the sculptor. In every work of art the artist takes his material from nature or experience and translates it into his medium, creating in it, as he works, something that was not there before. His creation is partly in terms of his material and partly in terms of the medium employed. Our consciousness of the medium is a part of our perception of a work of art and of our pleasure in it. One among the many reasons why Velasquez is a great painter lies in the distinction with which the paint itself is a part of his work: the texture, the brush, the density of the painting medium, and the color as well are a part of the idea that Velasquez's picture presents. In Shakespeare, at his best, along with the dramatic emotion and the thought we have always a sense of words being employed, of sheer phrasing and diction, as a part of our delight. Something of the truth of an Egyptian statue is in the granite of it.

In the director's use of his actors it ought to be true that the more he can use in his scheme of the play the actor's own stuff, the better. The different truths of a great sculpture in wood and a great sculpture in marble will consist partly of the difference between wood and marble. It ought to be the fact that a certain deepening in the truth of an actor's contribution to a play will derive from the actor's getting his results in terms of himself, making up out of his own elements the result that he creates. It will allow a better chance for those explosive accidents that we call inspiration, those moments when the actor is carried beyond his own plan or clear intention. At such moments a certain unexpected contribution to the director's creation may come from the medium itself, which may contribute to his invention, give him an idea. Many an architect has got a design, a motive, a form, from some quality of texture, color, or weight of the stone that he is using. The limitations of marble may invite no little of the sculptor's pattern. This might be called keeping the medium alive. The director brings the actor's own truth to the creation of the larger truth that the director is after.

If, for example, then, you have, as in Lenormand's *Les Ratés*, a scene in which a crude black man is brought suddenly to the discovery of a corpse and cries aloud, it ought to be true that the first thing to do is to let the actor make the cry himself, express his own kind of emotion in his own kind of cry, and then to use all this as far as possible rather than to start by explaining the emotion and giving him a cry to imitate. If an actor, rehearsing for the storm scene in *King Lear*, feels a certain way in the part, the director may use this feeling as far as he can toward the creation of the feeling that he himself wishes to express. He must believe that his actors are souls as well as bodies, and that the creation he seeks is composed of all our human elements. In sum, such a use of the actor medium by the director ought to be the means of keeping his performance alive in all its parts, as a good painter keeps the paint or a good sculptor keeps the marble alive in every inch of his surface.

SOPHOCLES' GUEST

SOPHOCLES' GUEST

THERE is no doubt a young man somewhere who might very well go to see *Œdipus Rex* at one of those classical revivals of the play in Athens. And the brunt of the play's mind on him and the power of Greek thought and life might set up something like a conversion, for a time at least, and divert him into new but yet old and habitable ways.

He is an American youth, grown up in an average town; he has an honest, active life in him and a certain readiness of motion in numerous directions. He is typical but not average. His nerves are keen, his brain alive; and in the midst of him is something that is busy, half troubled, and a little wistful. He has known no society in any large sense, only the unit that the family is—and that an unsettled unit nowadays—and a series of parties and entertainments by which people tend to bring themselves more or less together. The natural world he has lived with healthily, excursions, walks, and games, and sometimes with a shy poignancy and dream in his heart at the aspect of nature's beauty and growth and mystery. At college he was not wholly usual, since he studied and read. And he came out of college with what is not to him a satisfactory amount of information, loyalties, concessions, borrowings, and thwartings of his nature. He knows that there is something that he wants more of; what that something is, exactly, remains intense but vague. Despite his father he knows, at least, that he wants to write; he wants to express the life he sees; he sees the swarm and flow of American life, he reads the publicities of the American press about the theatre, and he wants to write plays.

The young man believes that energy and movement will carry him through, and that in these terms he can grapple with life and out of it create an art. And yet, behind this energy and faith in acquisition, he is restless; he drives and wheedles and bites at life. He is hungry for himself. He is perpetually taking himself to pieces without knowing just what is the design into which he is trying to put himself together again.

Without believing anything very clearly this man is a strong believer. He is not poetic in the traditional sense of the word in English societies; he is for something more active perhaps than he conceives poetry to be. Not poetic, perhaps, not willing to let the quietness and lure of romantic meditation take its way with him, or to make his dream a passion. But he is enthusiastic; he thinks that life can be made to express him. He sows himself on life, which is the poet working in him, after all.

Of science this young man knows a good deal; he had in college waves and fads of it, mixed in with philosophy and personal fashions in psychology and the social theories of the day. He has still a certain laboratory cockiness about small facts that seem to him incontestably supported by investigations, however small. In religion he has fads likewise, is prepared for anything, the news of a dozen new cults a year. Of the soul's journalism he is a busy and well-posted subscriber. But in general he holds to his father's religion and rebels against it when he chooses; that constitutes his religious activity, so far as one sees it, though he has his mystery there too. And what he knows most about of late years is the science, the psychology and religion of sex. He and his fellows have read the new and old books on that subject; they consider themselves experts upon it, and are open to every comer, every explanation, disenchantment, or inspiration. Psychoanalysis is the handmaid of his raids in such research. In politics he has certain notions of the game. His thoughts are tinged with a suggestive but not dangerous socialism. He has heard much of social service, of universal brotherhood, the outlawry of war, and normalcy, whatever that may be. In conceptions and general ideas he cannot be said to have laid his ground very spaciously. He has a vast mixture of theories, points of view, creeds, and systems. He has never met with ideas around and about him to any extent. Perhaps the most nearly inclusive idea he has is that of uniformity. Not conformity; he would resent having to conform to any will or dictum; it is uniformity that he moves toward; he likes to have men and things one at bottom and going on from that one into all—in sum, he likes variety rather than difference. And yet he does not; and no one knows what wildness may be in his heart, though the American life around makes the release of it distasteful even to him.

But, whatever else this youth may be, he is racial in that he is an individualist. He is not always an individualist in an important sense, driving individualism into an idea; and not always impetuously an individualist. But he begins obstinately with himself. He is, in some odd way, his own authority, the editor of himself. He sees heaven with his own eyes, and they are his feet that tread and define whatever cosmic tracks he traverses. He sets out to think for himself and to take his own where he finds it. His mind is accordingly a rag-bag. Into it this notion and that, this thought or system or quotation, is received protestingly or eagerly but always personally, for he mistrusts order or rule or authority. He has little impulse, so far as he realizes, toward any but a personal arrangement and outlook on all life and all culture and thought. But as it leaps here and there his is a sensitive spirit, somewhat starved by the thinness of the life he has seen, and somewhat hurried and confused by the stream of his country and era. His wits are alive, and his eyes and legs wandering and avid.

He goes then to the play, down to the theatre of Dionysos, through the lively streets. By some happy arrangement the play will be given in the morning, with the bright light of the sun overhead, the country, the people set forth with the life of the morning on them. From the lines of the open theatre the eyes travel to the lines of the surrounding world, as they are led upward to the sky by the descending light. The play begins, not perfectly done, of course, not drilled enough, and lacking knowledge of how the Athenians of Sophocles' day carried through its various theatrical parts, through the recitation, dancing, chorus and so on, the statement of the theme. But behind the makeshift and the imperfections the old forms are shadowed nevertheless; and what the ancient order of thought and the ancient quality of beauty were is still to be discerned.

The play begins. The crowd enters, the people driven by pestilence toward their king and toward the gods. The prophet comes; a curse is on the land. Œdipus sets out upon the search that is to be his fate. Jocasta, ill-starred and violent, the woman who is his mother and also his wife, throws herself between Œdipus and this knowledge that will destroy them all. And finally in shame and frenzy Jocasta hangs herself, and Œdipus with the clasp of her mantle digs out his eyes. He enters then in that most terrible shudder in all drama; he feels the pain, his voice floats far from him, shame in this world and in the next he feels; all things, even his children, are taken from him, and he goes out to wander alone over the world. And meanwhile the chorus has sung and moved, and carried into a wider region the events of the play and the thoughts of the characters. The music of the instruments has widened yet further the whole, giving it a yet more general and essential abstraction, and seeming to spread upon it an aspect of the eternal. The changing lines of the chorus and the actors have rendered less obscure the poet's desire and all his thought; the Salamis or the inland wind, blowing another rhythm into those bright garments, has carried into universal space that flow of movement under the wide light.

The young man sits and sees and hears. All very well and very classical, no doubt, but a man thinks for himself. He has resisted at first. Life, he insists, is not so simple as all this. This story of Œdipus is moulded from without, it stood ready to Sophocles' hand; into this story the

characters are fitted, with their several parts to
bear and their functions to perform in a general
idea. And these characters are not people, they
are figures with vast outlines in some yet larger
outline. Through them, as through the story,
the forces play. This entire arrangement and
spectacle, the movements, the acting, the scene,
are not actual but as far away as the story and
the figures in it. The young man tells himself
that if you simplify life in this fashion you are
avoiding the point and problem of it. But gradually, nevertheless, something has happened; it
is as if the landscape had sunk into him. He
begins to have within him the sense of a long,
deep vista, a clearness, an impersonal ascent.
And at length he walks away in the midst of the
crowd, who are discussing the play and the performance of it with such volubility.

Hours pass as he walks about the streets;
for, by some persuasion new to his mind, the
thoughts he has must be carried through to
their conclusion publicly. They must be thought
among thoroughfares of men, and not in those
places that he sees stretching far off into the
country, leading their quiet planes in the soft
light and under lengthening shadows. He thinks

of Leonardo da Vinci's phrase that he has wondered about at home, "how sweet the people's
faces in the streets," and for the first time it
seems simple and without sentiment to him.
How sweet the people's faces that he sees passing by in the streets, how open and gentle life
seems in them! And then, as he must do if he is
not to be a traitor to his race, he goes back to
his own room and closes the door. He sits down
by the open window, settles himself, and, in a
way that makes us love his kind, he takes stock.

The world, it seems, if we listen to Sophocles
and his classical art, consists for us of our ideas
as they arise, survive, complete themselves.
There are many things that we do not understand in the universe, in life, in ourselves. But
we may have a sense of a line, perhaps, of a scope,
a continuity. We may not understand anything
at all in itself, but we can see its relation to other
things in our world of living and ideas. And we
can move toward ideas, conceptions, in which
many things take their places. We may discover, evolve, and create patterns, images, symbols, conceptions. Is it possible, he begins to ask
himself, that some kinds of living are more
representative, more inclusive of all life? And

would the art therefore that expressed such living have a form that might remain significant and seem to include or comment on the rest of life?

The young man hurls himself about; a great force has taken him. He will never be at home in this classical world of thought, of art, of life, he knows; but he knows, too, that he should not be, since he is an American and not a Greek of Sophocles' time. Other kinds of art, he knows very well, are good, also; they have each one its necessity for existence. His brain tells him that every kind of living must find the expression closest to it; Strindberg for the life he expresses, Chekhov for his, Ibsen, D'Annunzio, Bernard Shaw. And yet he is held; Sophocles has made an inroad on him.

As for these ideas, these permanent forms and conceptions within which Sophocles sets his drama and his comment on living, the young man reminds himself that in the natural world around us what survives and reappears is form, idea, not the dust that goes to the making of every tree and beast. Nature constantly approximates finalities, forms within which life may complete and express itself forever. Why not likewise in the realm of human living and thought? Aye, aye, forms of living, forms of thought, in which our human life completes and expresses itself forever.

As he sits there brooding he is suddenly disarmed by recognizing what has been the direction of late that he himself and his friends have taken when in their criticism of life they draw on science. He remembers how often one said these days that this man was in such and such a class physiologically, biologically; how often one has only to say of some one that he is that sort of man, as if to make every excuse for him or explanation necessary. He remembers how much the theories of punishment and crime, of prisons and schools, turn nowadays not on individuals in themselves so much as on the characteristics and forces that make them what they are and make them act as they do. And all that, he realizes, is taking a Greek point of view, all that turns on forces that exist in nature and work in individuals. Science and visitation of forces, of gods! In the human body the visitation and shock of universal elements! We may have the will to suppress and repress and control; but the forces come; if at no other time, they possess our dreams, gods coming in dreams to man! The young man's father would have denied that; such a point of view would have insulted character, will, morality and Queen Victoria. Not so with the young man and his friends; they were ready to receive the light. And here in Greek the same thinking went on. But it moved not so much toward relaxations and the loosening of standards as toward outlines, forms, the sense of ideas into which contributing details took their relative place.

It was like those charts of mariners that lead to conceived and desired ends, to harbors and over tracks that have been plotted out. Under these lines of purpose and direction lies the sea, a ceaseless, ungoverned passion of energy and eternal power, an unfathomed and inexhaustible mystery of being, a boundless vitality and danger. But the chart remains and man's navigation may be informed by it. There are ports foreseen and attainable for the voyage that he must make, no matter what his will is or the weariness and perplexity of his heart. The art, or the thinking, that follows such a conception is by its own nature driven to find its charts and possible ways. It plots out, above the immense and inexhaustible sources of human nature and living, an order, a plan, a course in art that will bring us to rational and sweet harbors, and into ports and havens from which we may look out over the ocean with some consolation of understanding. A man's life, then, under this Greek scheme, moves perpetually through the expression and the discipline of it toward a large and grave and foreseen outline, a beautiful and persuasive design. Under this Greek scheme a man respects in art lucidity and easy and consummate statement and the recreative power of clear light; he doubts the virtue of that which groaning or skilful confusion or poignant chaos may stumble upon. To him art must be passionate and universal, but the born heir of a divine and tranquil nature.

Sex, in this Sophoclean world, the young man perceives, was less diverting and curious and detailed. It was admitted, simply, completely, but left in a larger relationship; it was not so personal, not so special. He remembers, too, with a start, that modern thought is about to take away time, and now perhaps to deny even motion, leaving only relationships in space—

a universe all pattern, all design, that would be, would it not? Would it not?

Suddenly his American uniformity appears to be a small thing. It is only a poor version of conformity after all. That a race of men should contemplate the same ideas—love, justice, say—with a view toward the progress, clarity, and completion of them, might be a fine thing. That all men should be expected to agree to certain conceptions or applications of these ideas—love, justice, say—is stupid, narrow and mediocre. To the young man sitting there at his Athens window this thought is a shock. He begins to ask himself if belief is merely personal, stubborn, insistent. But, on the other hand, aside from believing, there is much to see, to apprehend, to remain open to, to build and perfect. His body does not live only by what it attacks, bites, adopts, chews up, makes it own. It lives also by what rests on no personal determination at all, by the healthful light, the respiration of his lungs, and the beating of his heart that sends the blood—whose crimson is magnificent in his eyes whenever he meets it in the world—through his veins. How foolish it would be, he starts suddenly and decides, to set up a dogma, a belief about the beating of his heart! But how wisely he may try to conceive what forces are behind that pulse in it! It is necessary, he decides at this moment, not so much to consider good and bad, sins and virtues, but rather an excellence and the defect of an excellence; to contemplate forces. It is necessary not to make these so special and personal, for anger may be evil or righteous, passion may make a profligate or a saint, beauty may make or destroy, and so on; let them be forces whose nature we study and whose wise application to life we seek.

The race behind this classic art of Greece, the young man reflects, was at home in the world. But it was not at home in the same way that he had been, restlessly optimistic, confident that things could be made to work. There may be something in that, if you will; but after Sophocles it seems only an adolescent courage and evasion. This at-homeness of the Greeks arose from other things, from a lively and keen-eyed response to the world and observation of it, and a sense of fatalità, as the Italians call it—fatality, though that is too depressing a word for it—destiny, though that word is too dark. As for the young man, he understands from his heritage of religious philosophy a kind of mysticism, a resignation before the will of God, a kind of Christian, Oriental, mediæval abnegation of self. But he sees that this Greek fatality is an idea arising from an experience with the universe that has confronted the universe with the human mind and has perceived what appear to be processes working in their due courses and including man with them. Before these man does not prostrate himself, mystically offering his death and ecstasy; but rather tries to recognize and give them place. And he secures his home in the world by accepting these forces as he takes the rain and sun; and he secures his intelligence by admitting their existence and operation.

The young man thinks of the life he has known in America. That life, he knows, has simplified itself and lost much of an old, long world culture. The wholesale methods by which ideas are sent broadcast into men's minds, and the reduction of all ideas to a popular accessibility and simplicity, what do they promise for American life? Is it moving toward a certain large outline? Something more single? The beginning of a new myth, more elemental, final, universal?

But for such ends to attain to any importance or significance there would have to be not merely a simplification of life and popular culture toward less complexity, but a simplification toward essentials. Intelligence, effort, time, would be needed for that, if it is ever to come. His thought travels to the theatre. How far are we tired of photography, of accidental living, of things with a false plausibility to them that satisfies the comfortable and commonplace? How far is our theatre tired of recognizing that a chair is a chair, and that there are four legs to a horse? How far do we move toward larger ideas in our theatre, however simple and lacking in finality our statement of them might be? And will these ideas, will this American life find itself in dramatic forms, forms suited to embody the precise soul of the matter? Could a general outline of dramatic thought arise, true to our living, and, though not yet a great universal form, at least free of elements not its own? He wonders.

But when all else is said and done, there is one thing in Sophocles that sticks in the young man's craw; he will not admit the characters as they are in this drama. Men to him are individuals, each with his peculiar ways, his personal traits,

his twists and turns; our whole racial tradition of an individual starts with these private
details. Sophocles' people, he objects obstinately within himself, are not persons at all,
this so-called Œdipus and Jocasta and Creon.
They, too, are only types, outlines, they move in
forms, they are created of only ideal substance.
According to this classical art, he discerns, the
centre of a man is universal, not private. Man
takes his glory from all glory, he embodies rather
than evolves it. Man is most himself, Sophocles
says, when he is most universal; universal not by
some mystical ecstasy and sense of entrance into
the heart of God, as the youth in his quieter
hours has thought or has read in the sayings
here and there of saints, but by some more or
less completion in himself of ideas, enduring conceptions, parallels of the continuous in human
experience.

And yet what is it in these characters, in
Tiresias, Œdipus, Jocasta, that moves him so?
Is it only certain living ideas, permanent forces
in human living, passion, wisdom, anger, he-
redity, beauty? The shock of these in men's
minds, and in this poet's especially, drove images
into being. These great images, Œdipus, Jocasta,

and the rest, arise out of the power that the idea has to work creation in men's minds. Out of the idea these heroic shapes are born. The young man broods on these great tragic personages. These characters do not limit him, in them he walks and finds himself, the terror and magnificence of what a man is; and he is not one but all of them. It is as if in some heroic music his own heart heard its beating.

The boy is troubled about himself, his character, his individuality. This personality of his that he has thought so much about, seems detailed enough but without design. One cannot, he thinks at this moment, be personal, individual, different, except by comparison with ideas, with qualities; and the importance of one's difference or individuality lies in the importance of what the comparison involves. He has inherited—no doubt, he reflects—the impulse to proceed from within outward in his apprehension of the world; he has, if you like, a certain special, intricate, emotional, even violent, centre; but what is it the centre of?

He smiles to think that he might be immersed once more again in one of the old college arguments around the fire.

And now it appears to him that much of his
northern poetry only moons and mystifies and
strays; its supposed divinity is only confusion
or certain special words that open into mists and
eternities. He reflects how much the people he
had known had carried into their love of nature,
about which they talked so much, had carried
into the woods, clouds, streams that they practised, only an instinct for losing themselves in a
green vapor, of making an evasion of themselves.
How often had he tended to elude and tremble
before his own nature !

The memory comes into his mind of the wood
where he used to wander when he was in college.
It was a wood on little slopes of ground, with
streams sometimes seen, sometimes covered with
leaves and moss and dead boughs. There was a
thick undergrowth sometimes, and sometimes
only weeds and tangled vines; the vista of the
wood was uneasy and blurred, cut across and
scratched over with twigs and every age of trees.
For a season he had busied his walks in this
wood with learning the notes of birds, with seeking new ferns, and spelling out their species to
the last letter. But later he had reverted to
walking merely, wandering, almost always alone.

And now he thought of his walk in Athens yesterday. He had gone down along the Ilyssus and then to the Eleusis road. The ground for the most part was clear, the stream shone within its low banks. There were oleanders there, blossoming white; there were laurels, and ilexes now and then, a few plane-trees and pines, and sometimes a cypress. Along the road to Eleusis, as he passed the hill where Kolonos once stood, there came a goatherd leading his beasts and playing a shepherd's pipe. The pipe rose like a deathless voice clearly toward the clear light.

In the wood at home, the young man remembers, his thoughts had not been anywhere in particular, but he had found his being rested and soothed. He had come home from those walks in many moods, muddled, lifted, desperate with the shadow of vague yearning everywhere. He had felt in his heart a shy tenderness, and even among his companions afterward a kind of blunt lyricism. Sometimes he had had a sense of a something everlasting, something in him, too, that would never die, however much the tired self might want to shuffle off this mortal coil— jolly old phrase! Sometimes he had felt religious, the mystery of the universe had seemed to minister to him. He had felt a sense of God, an infinite soft mist within, like a faint music heard and lost at the same time. He wondered now about that religion and about his preoccupation sometimes with religion. How much of that was mere insistent details in egoism? And what about conscience? That beloved conscience—was conscience only devil-worship, after all? If you saw the values in things and knew to what end your choice among various courses of living was to be made, you might regret your folly, weakness, or stupidity, you might suffer in your conscience perhaps, but always and only for a reason. Too personal an affair with religion made for sentimentality, scrupulosity, eccentricity, inconsequence. Or did it?

Along that clear road through the burned, harsh, yellow, and violet land, with the rocks, the sudden, black pines, the little shaded groves, he had gone yesterday and had returned at length through the teeming streets to his own room. About all this there had been a sense, first of all, of shapes and spaces, and of the eye recognizing its own judgment and power and delight. There had been the stretch of ground, the outline of an ilex-tree, the silver of the stream, even the precision of the laurel and oleander leaves. He had not thought of God at all, he had not been filled, comforted. That undying shapes and images had arisen in his mind he knew, deities, immortal figures of the various world. The clear outlines of trees; the infinite light upon the ground and over all things; the certainty and transparency of shadows; the columns of marble set against the sky; the ground near by, the vista toward the hills and the inland country; time, ascent and descent, the due rhythm and course of things—he had felt a sense of permanency not within himself, not within his own mystery, but in that part of himself that lived in those forms and qualities that appeared to him in the world around him there. He had felt the sense, not of being quiet in some mystical eternal arms or of being stirred with some unrest, but of moving toward some perfection. And if then, along Ilyssus and in that clear light, he had thought of God at all, it would have been as of some Ultimate Mind by which, if he could know Him, all things among themselves might be perceived. God, then, he reflects—knowing that he could never free himself of the word—might be a kind of antiphonal radiance of all things among themselves, by which alone their truth appears.

The boy sits there by his window looking out on the mountains, Lykabettos, and the long slopes of Pentelicos, and the country around. The light lies yellow on them, on the walls of the town; the Bay of Salamis stretching to the southwest grows darker and bluer. The lines of this world he looks upon are clear and final; they establish a final relationship together. He feels a still and lucid power among his thoughts, as if life were all pure space seen in the light and music of his contemplation. And sitting there he sees the wonderful night come on. Over the sad land he sees the stars rise. And to-night at least, watching them in the clear heavens and the forms they take, he thinks not on the mystery but on the pattern of his soul.